D1693497

VORMATOR
the elements of design

booreiland   zeptonn

Foreword

Foreword from the Editors

How it all began…

It was a cold and dark winter eve, at the end of the year 2006 when Wimer and Jan Willem were enjoying a simple home-cooked Italian dinner. While wrestling with the pasta, they were discussing how creating music and graphic design were alike: both are composed of separate elements that can often be reorganized (or remixed) later. Also there are several layers in a piece, and perfection often lies in small details.

This reminded Wimer of an experimental music project that he performed in which a group of people received the same set of samples and one basic challenge: create a song. Depending on the skills and styles of the people involved, a wild range of interesting, surprising, weird and some beautiful songs where the result.

Because visual artists are often challenged by limitations in a similar way as music creators, Wimer and Jan Willem questioned themselves: Why not try and organize a similar challenge for the field of graphic design and illustration? Imagine what would happen when artists contribute graphics stripped down to their essence. Would their work still be strong and recognizable? What would artists, both established and upcoming talent, come up with under imposed restrictions?

And so, somewhere in between anti-pasta and dessert, an idea was born that eventually became known as Vormator.

To maximize the effect of limitations Wimer and Jan Willem introduced a limited set of shapes to be used under strictly supervised rules. The challenge for each artist would be to create a one-page piece by using only these shapes within the set of given rules. The project was not only intended to challenge artists, but also to show the importance of limitations in creative work.

As it goes these days, the internet played a major part in distributing the Vormator challenge all over the world. Little did we know that we would receive close to six-hundred submissions to choose from! From Paris to Sao Paolo, from the USA to Tokyo, submissions flew in from everywhere.

As much as we love the internet, it cannot compete with the touch and smell of a well designed book. Therefore we decided to publish Vormator as book. In this book you will find a selection of what we think are the best of the submissions, showcasing a variety of solutions and working methods.

By letting the artists themselves explain their working methods and progress, we hope that you as a reader will be able to gain insight into how limitations can stimulate creativity. We hope that we have shown that, even with a large number of restrictions and few 'samples' to start with, a huge variation of graphics is still possible. Besides, unbridled access to resources is not always the way to go in design (or in life, for that matter)! We truly hope that you will enjoy reading this book as much as we did organizing the challenge and putting together the publication.

Sincerely,

Booreiland & Zeptonn

Booreiland is:
Menno Huisman & Wimer Hazenberg
info@booreiland.nl | www.booreiland.nl

Zeptonn is:
Jan Willem Wennekes
info@zeptonn.nl | www.zeptonn.nl

Thanks to:
André Weenink
Eelke Dekker | www.eelkedekker.nl
All artists that contributed to Vormator!

BISPUBLISHERS

Introduction by Von Glitschka

How limitations influence the process of creativity

History itself is replete with examples of human ingenuity showcasing it's creativity when faced with restrictive resources. So much so that a popular saying has survived a millennia and is still in use today to describe such situations. You have probably heard it.

"Necessity is the mother of invention."

When I first started out in this industry I thought the most creative assignment you could possibly have is one that had a huge budget affording you to do anything you wanted. You know, the sky's the limit and all that. Unfortunately that didn't prove itself to be true.

As my career proceeded and reality kicked in, I was faced with projects that had small to no budgets and yet I was still expected to find a unique creative solution for them. I found out pretty fast and it's been proven over the years that creativity is often fostered in the midst of sparse resources or time.

When you think about why this is you can isolate the possible reasons. When someone possesses abundance they have less needs in general. Proportionate to this abundance, is the tendency to have less motivation and creativity to meet the remaining needs they still have yet to gain. In a nutshell, they take their work for granted.

Instead of being unique problem solvers, they become participants in the status quo. You know the type "Just get it done and out the door." That element of creative challenge to accomplish something usually isn't there.

A person who possesses little tends to make good use of what they do have, and seeks to find new ways they can stretch it to accomplish more then what is expected. The creative challenge is paramount in exercising creativity to solve problems, and when that happens you tend to get something profoundly simple, yet simply profound.

There are those moments in the creative process when you're brainstorming ideas and stumble upon that precious jewel of inspiration. Doing this in the midst of scant resources and time is unfortunately becoming more rare as our industry moves at light speed into the digital realm. But as you'll see, it can be done and it doesn't take unlimited resources, it takes unlimited creativity and proves once again that necessity is the mother of invention.

The Vormator project has capitalized on this concept. Rather than letting mere chance force the issue, it has provided specific limitations (Vormator shapes) and the rules of engagement and handed them over to a variety of artists to see what they could create when faced with restrictive perimeters.

So turn the pages and marvel at the brilliant ideas birthed from limitation.

Von Glitschka

Von Glitschka is *a freelance Illustrative Designer who is very active in the design world. Along his illustrative design work, Von pursues an insane number of other design interests. He teaches digital illustration at a local college. He also created and runs www.illustrationclass.com, a resource site for students and professional alike. He writes numerous articles and tutorials for websites and magazines, such as Computer Arts. Von has also spoken at a number of conference about the creative process. Von has worked in the communications arts business since 1987 and started his own design firm in 2002. Von lives in Salem, Oregon, U.S.A. with his wife Rebecca, and has two creative daughters, Savannah and Alyssa.*

You can find *out more about Von Glitschka and his work on his website, www.glitschka.com.*

Meet the Elements

The Zerk

This stocky guy is as passive as they come. Chronic depressed as he is, the Zerk has a hard time living. He spends many nights in the dark, watching late night TV for hours. He has become entirely apathetic due to the materialistic world. Often being pushed around and taken advantage of by the other Elements, he has no strong sense of self-confidence. He has a crush on the Drop, and secretly hopes that she is willing to be his light at the end of the tunnel. A sad guy indeed.

The Drop

This emo-chick has a borderline personality. Her stylish and elegant looks have made many victims, something that she is completely unaware of. She is the only one that really knows how to appreciate the music that the Badge and his band makes, and is horrified by the fact that it is used in the erotic film industry. She is quite unstable, and her mood can swing from happy to sad or angry in just a matter of seconds. A simple remark can throw her off easily.

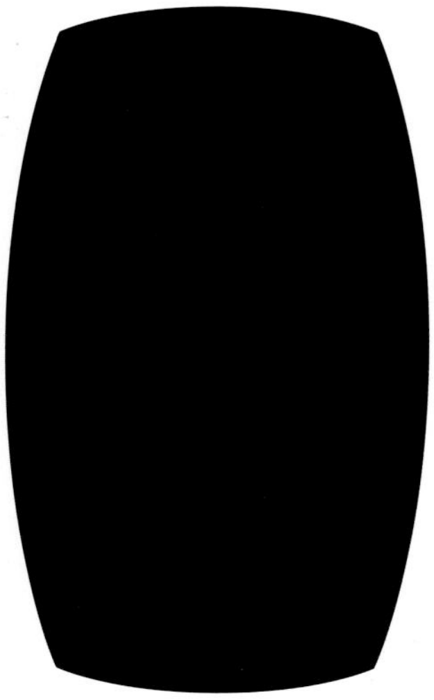

The Bar

This guy is not someone to mess around with. The Bar is daring and strong, and is not particularly known for his intelligence. With brute force he will make sure that he gets what he wants, although he can be very smooth and slick as well. He can easily be bribed with large amounts of German Beer, which he will drink down in no time. It will be no surprise to learn that this broad-shouldered guy has a criminal history, and has spent several years in prison. For all the machismo surrounding him, no one knows that he has had strong sexual feelings for Le Chevron for years that he never dared to express in public.

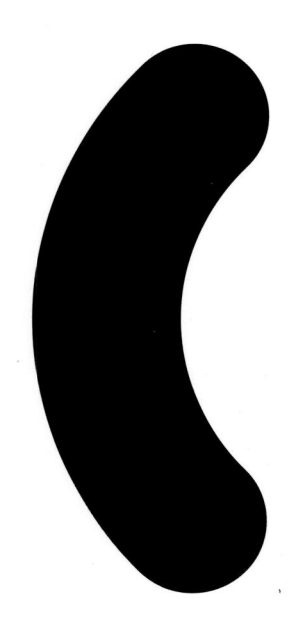

The Wurst

The Wurst has an awful sense of humour. He likes corny and stereotypical jokes, and has many prejudices about the other Elements. He wants to be in control, and gladly lets others do his work for him. He often pushes the Tentacle to mess around with the other Elements, and gladly watches the fights that arise from such situations. At night he abuses his good but fleshy looks to get his will. Watch out for this Australian-born dude, because he will return no matter what.

The Badge

After having worked as a sheriff for the larger part of his life, the Badge decided to take up his musical ambitions and became a guitar player in a hippie-band. He is the sensitive type, and often seeks comfort in the warm embrace of the Drop. Notwithstanding their artistic ambitions, the band's music has great success in the soft-erotic film industry.

The Chevron

A former militant in the army, the Chevron has a strong sense of leadership and continuously executes well laid-out plans. Hence, the Chevron was known as Chevron Guevara, or Le Chevron, back in the day. However, after having disciplined a number of followers in a gruesome manner, he was demoted. The Chevron now works as a parking guard in France. With his strong sense of authority and order, he is the one who strictly ensures that the Vormator rules are being applied correctly.

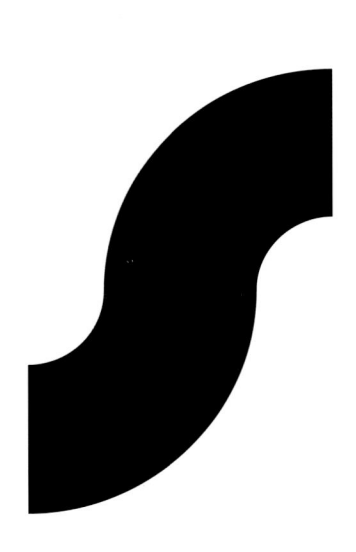

The Cobra

The Cobra has an artistic background, but has never had much success in that field. Forced to seek his prosperity elsewhere, he has worked as a maintenance guy in both the racing industry and the railroad system. Often distracted by flute-playing men, he never wanders around at the same location for a long time, but is always on the move. He is considerably intangible, and has a gift for replication. Recently though, the Vormator team has managed to trace his steps to the Fleischmann Factory, where he was found in a confused state.

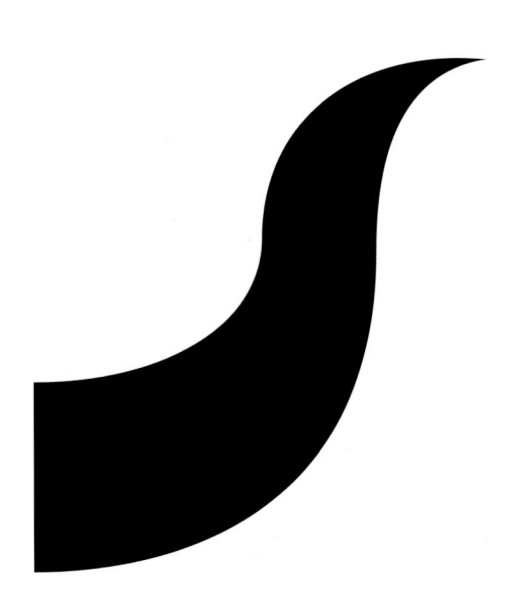

The Tentacle

The Tentacle is the mysterious one. She cannot be trusted, as her appearance can be very deceptive. As flexible as she is, she is able to adapt to many circumstances and will always make sure that she gets the best out of the situation. With her sharp sense of seduction, and her sleek sensual profile, she will never miss the opportunity to lure others in to her dark plans. She is also notorious for her habit of secretly tickling other Elements. Be warned, because she has a hand in much more than you might suspect.

The Rules

The Rules

What you can and cannot do with the Elements...

Vormator is the ultimate challenge of your creativity: the aim of the book is to give each artist the chance to show his abilities to create a stunning piece with limited means. The contributing artists each get the exact same set of 8 shapes, the Elements. With these shapes they are challenged to create their own unique page for the book, within the limitations provided in the Rulebook. Designers are thus challenged to create a unique piece within a strict set of rules. It all comes down to pure skills and creativity.

What exactly is allowed and isn't allowed with the Elements? The following rules have to be followed when creating the artwork:

1. Elements can be rotated, flipped and duplicated.
2. Not all Elements have to be used.
3. Scaling is allowed, but only proportionally, so no skewing or free transform.
4. Elements can be added, substracted, intersected and grouped with each other.
5. The use of colour is unrestricted.
6. Gradients are allowed.
7. The Elements may only be filled, the use of strokes is not allowed.
8. Filters or effects (e.g. drop shadows) are not allowed.

With these limitations in place each contributor will face the same challenge. Contributors will be selected based on their submissions, in other words: everybody will be judged by his/her true creativity. The rules will be applied strictly by the editors in the selection of artwork. The most important thing to bear in mind is that you are free to do as you see fit, as long as a viewer of the artwork is able to see that it is composed out of the Elements.

Selected Submissions

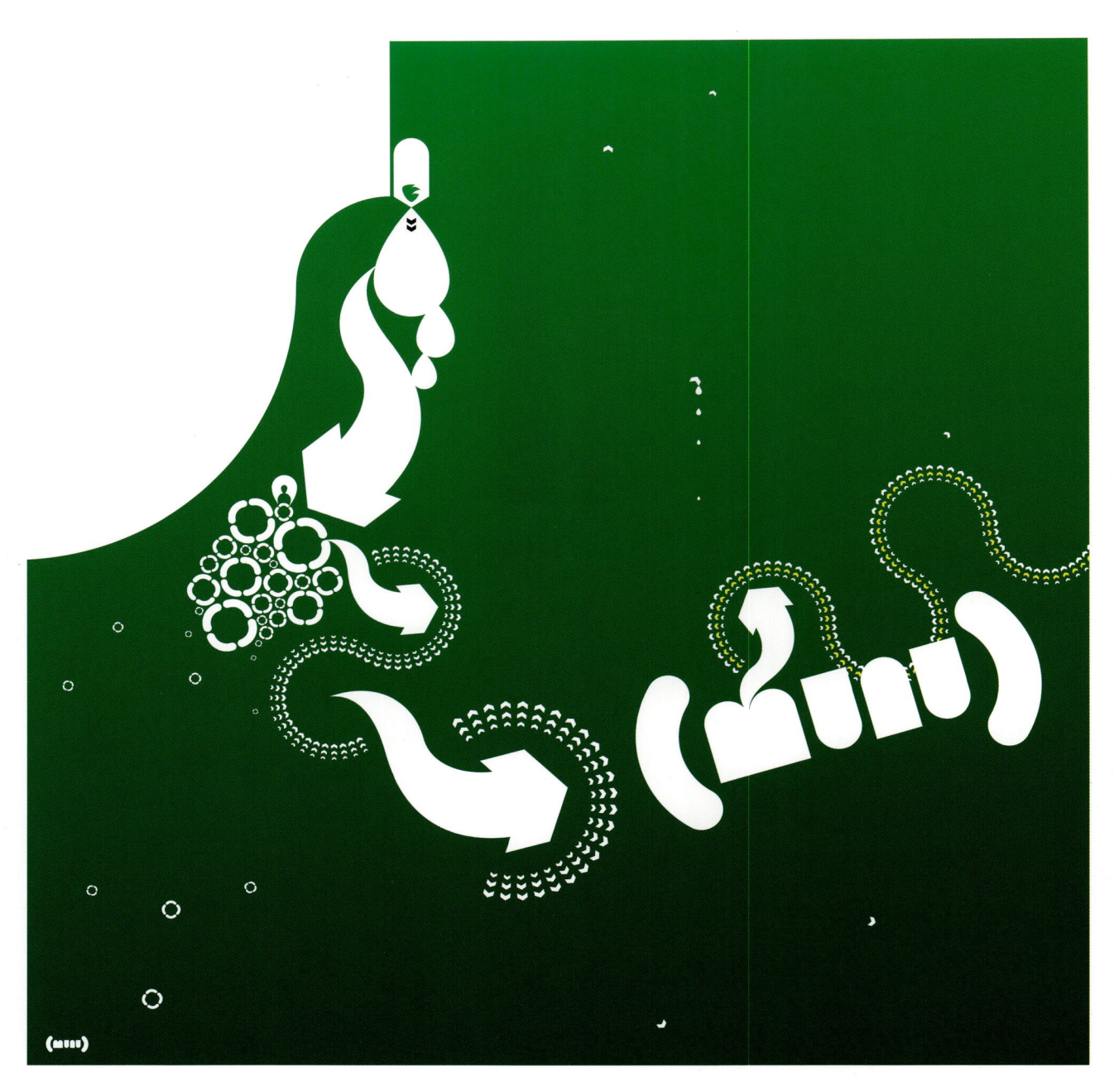

Mini

designer: 310K
location: Amsterdam, The Netherlands
website: www.310k.nl

310K IS THE *kind of guy who does a multitude of things. Of course he illustrates, but next to this magnificent job, he regularly lays his hands on VJ-sessions, gigs with his band and he organises vibrant events. His clients include MTV, Dance Valley and he has been involved with many other festivals. 310K has an odd but cheerful story about his inspiration and the construction of his piece.*

Shape 1
Base shape.

Shape 2
Construction object.

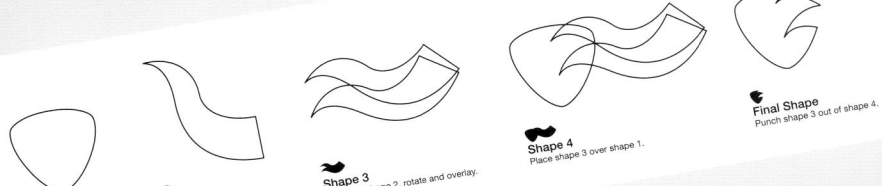

Shape 3
Duplicate shape 2, rotate and overlay.

Shape 4
Place shape 3 over shape 1.

Final Shape
Punch shape 3 out of shape 4.

The layout reminds me of my car, an old Mini Cooper. Just like the car, it rounds lots of corners, has a playful attitude and leaks when it rains. The green in this layout represents British racing green (even though my car is not this colour). Direction, movement, fun: me & my Mini.

At the start this design was blank – like my mind – and the Elements seemed to be thrown all over the page. I was looking for a focus point. Maybe it was a miserable rainy day in Amsterdam or maybe I was still a bit drunk from the night before – who knows? On the second day it changed into the colour red, probably when I got angry because the Elements weren't falling in the right places. On the third day I was feeling more relaxed. The abstract (Mini) icon popped onto the page and gave it confidence and a kind of cohesion. With this new direction and identity the colour changed to green.

The task was then to cut from the colour block using a selection

"Maybe I was still a bit drunk from the night before."

from the Elements. Most of the shapes in the layout are different from the given Elements. Creating these shapes was generally done by either combining Elements or subtracting Elements from each other. Repetition plays a big part in this layout, both randomly and conformed.

The illustration shows the process of my sweat dripping down in a few directions, forming shapes, going on again and again and finally coming to a conclusion. On the other hand: a connection between the great small car, the Mini, and British racing green cannot be ruled out.

Looking at and moving the Elements around was the beginning of the design process, just as it is with many projects I work on. Often a small part of one thing can trigger the rest to fall into place. Such choices do not always happen instantly and sometimes it is best to leave these scattered objects for a while and come back to them with a different frame of mind.

At the beginning of this project I struggled to find the motivation to get the ball rolling. Pushing on through several ideas I came to this, my favourite solution. I tend to say that this project did not change the way I approach design. It did however impose certain rules and guides, which is in line with the real world of being a graphic designer. In short the Vormator project was a good challenge.

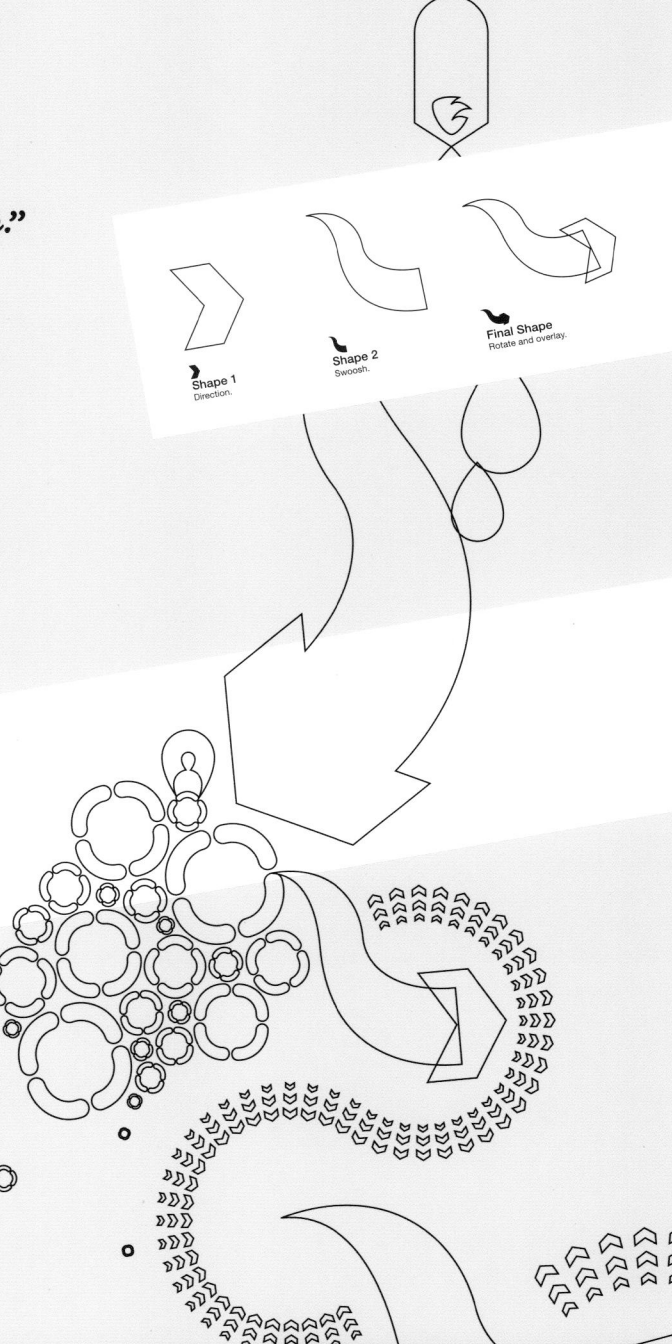

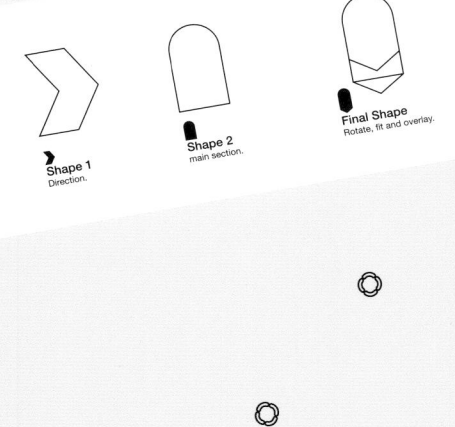

Shape 1
Direction.

Shape 2
Swoosh.

Final Shape
Rotate and overlay.

Shape 1
Direction.

Shape 2
main section.

Final Shape
Rotate, fit and overlay.

Who? is King

designer: Adam Turecek
location: Prague, Czech Republic
website: www.gngbng.com

ADAM TURECEK IS *32 years old and comes from the city of Prague in the Czech Republic. He is a student of Product design at the Academy of Arts and Design and currently works in a design studio. Besides product design Adam is interested in many things including street art, graphic design, badminton, fashion and of course – who isn't – sex. Keep that in mind while viewing his work.*

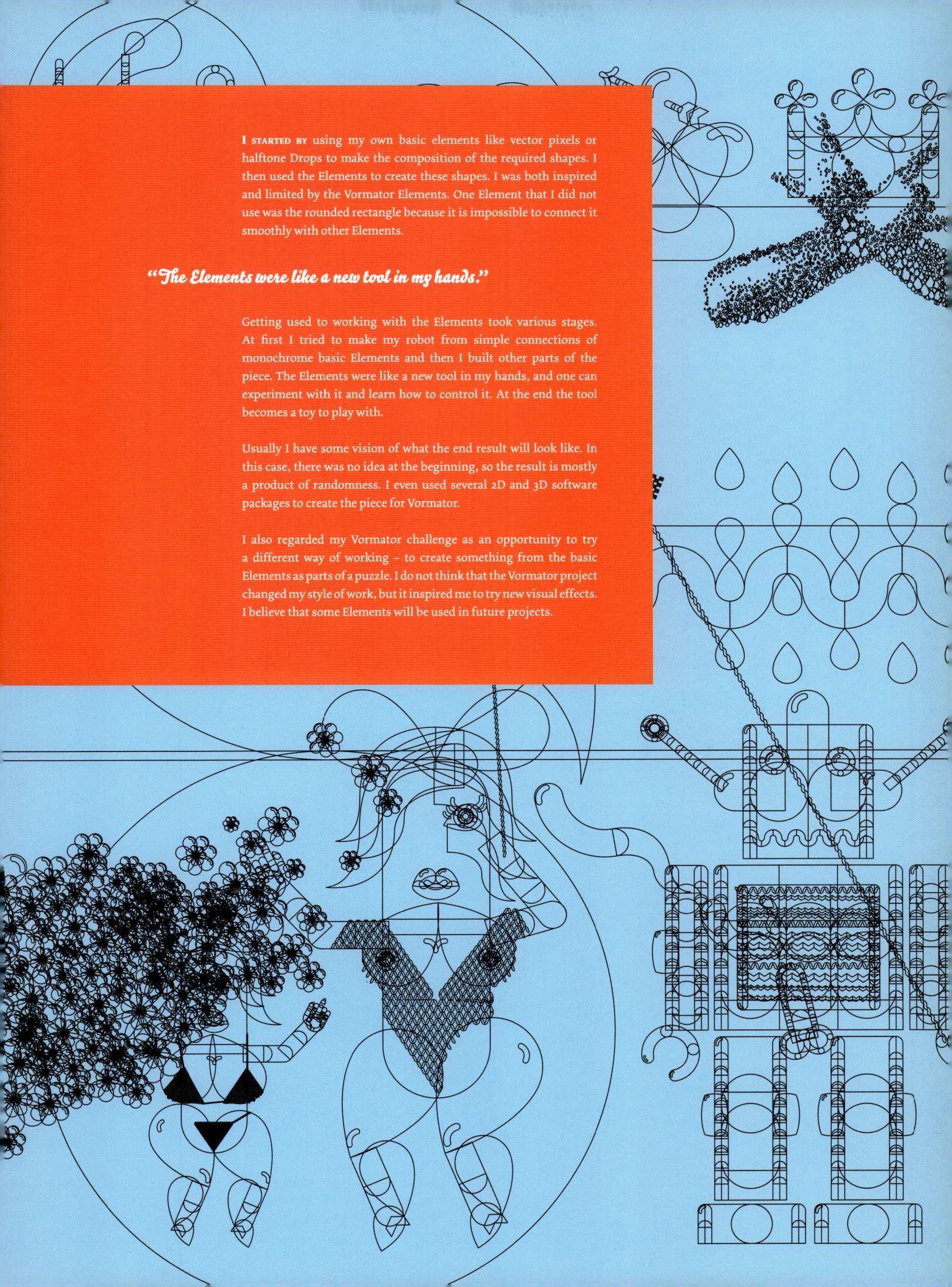

I started by using my own basic elements like vector pixels or halftone Drops to make the composition of the required shapes. I then used the Elements to create these shapes. I was both inspired and limited by the Vormator Elements. One Element that I did not use was the rounded rectangle because it is impossible to connect it smoothly with other Elements.

"The Elements were like a new tool in my hands."

Getting used to working with the Elements took various stages. At first I tried to make my robot from simple connections of monochrome basic Elements and then I built other parts of the piece. The Elements were like a new tool in my hands, and one can experiment with it and learn how to control it. At the end the tool becomes a toy to play with.

Usually I have some vision of what the end result will look like. In this case, there was no idea at the beginning, so the result is mostly a product of randomness. I even used several 2D and 3D software packages to create the piece for Vormator.

I also regarded my Vormator challenge as an opportunity to try a different way of working – to create something from the basic Elements as parts of a puzzle. I do not think that the Vormator project changed my style of work, but it inspired me to try new visual effects. I believe that some Elements will be used in future projects.

Ground State

designer: Hicalorie
location: Preston, UK
website: www.hicalorie.com

"...a giant silky furry mole mountain with a French accent."

Word Up! There is a Hicalorie in your pocket, but it's not one thing, it is many. Known by some as a collective of artists, by others as a brand, maybe a graffiti tag, a skate team, a clothing line or sometimes just a bunch of odd-but-lovable people, design outfit Hicalorie is built on a love for collaboration, cake, colours, coffee and creating things. Hicalorie has independently produced this and that, ranging from skateboards and speakers to tee shirts and toys, whilst also hosting and participating in art exhibits and group shows around the globe.

Designer Spotlight

DETERMINED TO SPLASH itself over every corner of the design spectrum, Hicalorie artwork has also been featured on album sleeves, magazine covers, art books, posters, illustrations, walls, benches, sneakers, boobies, clothing, animations, painted canvases, and toys.

THE ILLUSTRATION I created is a giant silky furry mole mountain with a French accent. The mole has audio speakers on its face to illustrate how, due to GM foods, most of today's moles are born blind so their other senses are heightened to match that of paranormal rodent super heroes.

The design was almost entirely made by simply grouping the Elements together to make new shapes and forms. It didn't turn out to be necessary to use all the Elements available to create the design; it would have actually caused more work to find a way to incorporate them all. So in a way, once a few new forms had been created, the limited number of Elements wasn't that restricting. There are also some fades and gradients in the design but these effects were used more for the sake of aesthetics and enhancing the colour pallet than to manipulate the look of the forms. Transparencies and subtle changes in colour were also very useful to make the forms more recognizable within the final design.

The whole process of creating the illustration was fairly ad lib. Working with the forms felt a lot like creating a collage rather than a typical illustration. So without any real experience working like that, the thing that felt most right to do was to just go for it. The basic outline originated from a rough pencil sketch, which was discarded after a few minutes, and the rest of the finished design is just the result of moving shapes aimlessly around on a monitor. The only real planned decision, which paid off, was to split the design into four layers, two foregrounds, a background and a far background, to avoid getting lost in a sea of tiny grouped Elements. This really helped towards the end when the file was getting so big that the computer seemed to be suffering from some kind of digital epilepsy.

Working on the Vormator challenge was very different compared to regular commission or illustration! To be deliberately given limitations to work with, rather than being assigned to a theme or subject, really had an effect on the design. I found it quite challenging trying not to constantly reach for the pen tool. For a while it seemed the thing to do was to try and overcome restrictions set by working the Elements and treating them as a hindrance. After a while though they definitely started to aid the design and add to it in a unique way, the design could be built very quickly by patterning the forms and experimenting with their placements. There were a few 'happy accidents' while working with the forms that definitely contributed to certain ideas. These wouldn't have been thought of otherwise.

The challenge definitely had a way of testing and encouraging lateral thinking while working on it. I'd expect most of the designs showcased in the Vormator project to have a unique aesthetic from the other works in their creators' portfolios. Maybe the collage and pattern techniques that Vormator encourages could be really useful to some designers or to actually inspire a style of design. I think I'll be reaching straight for the free form tool for a while though.

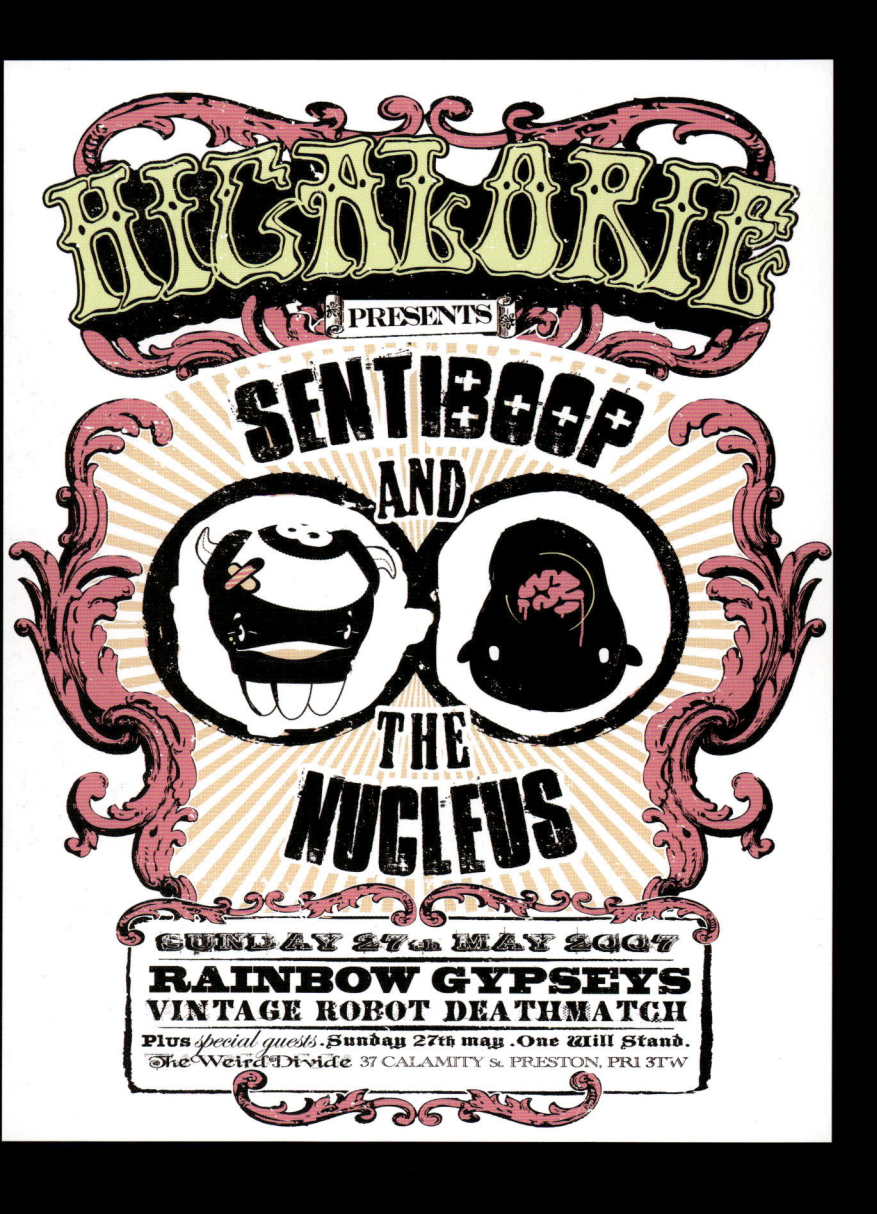

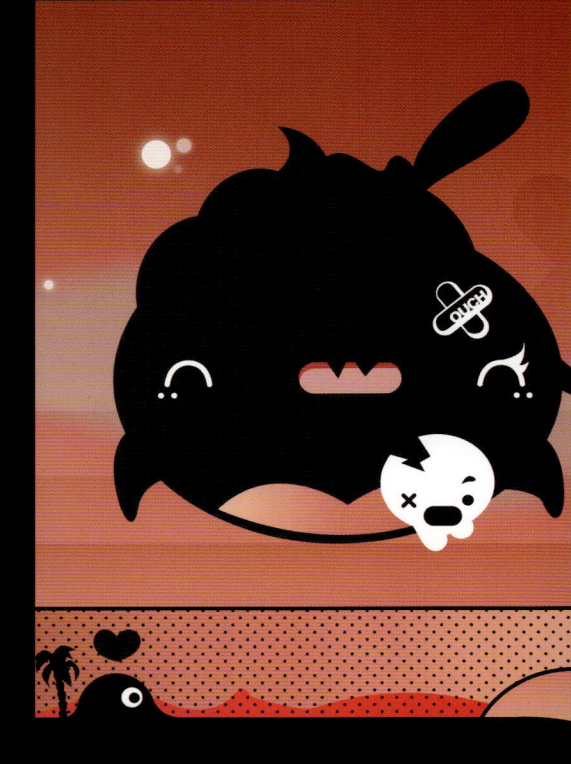

"I am happy to work in pencil the same way as I would a pen, Crayola®, spray can or whatever is lying around."

Generally when working alone working methods get very routine, pencil to Adobe® Illustrator®, Adobe® Illustrator® to Adobe® Photoshop® etc. I am not really fussy about tools so I am happy to work in pencil the same way as I would a pen, Crayola®, spray can or whatever is lying around, I am however a total Adobe® Illustrator® addict and rarely work without it. A lot of the work we do for Hicalorie is collaboration driven and so when an illustration involves a second set of hands it is fun to see how the working methods alter slightly. Sometimes it can be fairly challenging to work around someone else's methods, and other times it can be much more effective and insightful, but either way it seems to feel more interesting.

Illustration and character design are my sure favourites amongst the projects we do. However, most projects I have worked on this year were dramatically different from the previous ones, so I am still discovering a lot of new likes and dislikes.

I have always had a lot of art and design heroes since school, but I tend to keep them from becoming influences as such. If I listed my favourite artists or illustrators you'd probably see very little similarity between their work and mine, if any, partly because I wouldn't really want to borrow aesthetics from the artists I admire, but mostly because I usually appreciate artists with very stylized work or with skill sets that I just wouldn't even attempt to learn for fear of losing whatever is original about my own.

In my work I aim for plenty of smiles I guess. Although, having said that, usually when I draw this stuff I am rarely thinking about anything, or anyone, especially not about evoking some kind of reaction. Unless I have a particularly controlling client, I mostly just draw for myself and hope people like it.

Untitled

designer: Andy King
location: North East Lincolnshire, UK
website: www.mobobo.co.uk

ORIGINALLY TRAINED IN *Fine Art, specializing in sculpture, Andy King worked as a sculptural assistant and roadie for a number of years after finishing University. In 1994 he bought his first computer and embarked upon digital graphics production. Since teaching himself Adobe® Photoshop® in that year, he greatly enjoys utilising graphics and new media software to produce web sites, graphic design and illustration for a range of clients. Having worked for large, impersonal and as often as not unethical new media/computer companies he now does freelance work as well as writing and delivering courses in Higher Education. Andy likes to initiate production of digital graphics, illustrations, photography and animations for professional development and personal enjoyment.*

My intention was to explore the abstract possibilities of the interaction of the Elements, deliberately ignoring any specifically chosen subject. Despite this my output has a distinct figurative impact that could have its roots in a variety of sources: early video games; scrawled caricatures made in school notebooks; cave paintings. All of these, to a greater or lesser extent, added to a love of play with simple forms, gained when studying minimalist sculpture.

I wanted to use all of the Elements together once only – relying on the interplay between the Element's shape and blending to inform the composition. Any colours beyond shading an Element would have detracted from the visual impact of the forms, not allowing me to concentrate on how the shape informed itself in relation to the containing canvas and other Elements. I also restricted myself to using the Elements in their original form, without grouping or combining to create new shapes. Gradient fills and blending added to position, rotation and stacking of the Elements gave me more than enough scope with which to compose my output.

The development for this piece was a matter of, after having settled upon a layout, exploring the blending modes that best delivered my intentions for the Elements to influence one another in relation to the canvas.

The approach I take towards design for design's sake as opposed to that for paying clients is one of learning through play. Relaxing in front of the medium is a luxurious feeling that is usually swallowed by deadlines. The only real problem that I could, mistakenly, foresee was being unable to decide upon one composition. One tweak of an element: a rotation; gradient fill; scale or blending, would alter any arrangement having a domino effect on all others, leading to a vicious circle of change and indecision.

This brief has caused me to take stock of my early art influences and experiences, approaches and methodology, and reassess the possibilities they offer within my digital production techniques today. The Elements themselves are to me excitingly resonant of the communication graphic signs found saturating our daily environments, which I greatly enjoy and I wished to investigate within these simplified forms. The idea of communication via forms redolent of the Health and Safety nanny state dictatorial paternalism appealed to my cynical nature.

> *"One tweak of an element would alter any arrangement having a domino effect on all others."*

New Day

designer: Aras Atasaygin
location: Izmir, Turkey
website: www.xuppets.com

Aras Atasaygin was born in Turkey in 1986. His father is Iranian so he lives between Turkey and Iran. Living in different cultures determined his look on life. Aras spent his childhood in a village which, in this region, meant that he had lots of time for daydreaming. Ever since he had a pencil in his hand he has been doodling his imaginary friends. He loves colourful compositions and yummy forms. He loves mystic jelly ghosts, ninjas with chocolate sticks, girls in love with rabbits and all his imaginary characters that enter his brain every minute. He just wants to share them with you. Surprisingly though, he does not spend his time on studying art class. Instead he is in his third year of Economics and does his freelance illustration works as well.

"Each Element has a big potential to create new forms."

THE SUBJECT OF my piece is "new day". I tried to illustrate the rising of a new day which, to me, embodies hopes about the future, thinking about the persons you care for from the start of a day and difficulties that wait for you every day, like a boss! Life is not just positive or negative centric. It is something between these two and the best moment to describe this, is the sunrise.

Normally I begin with a sketch; a phase in which I try to find the best form for my elements. However, for this Vormator project I sat behind the PC straight away and tried to find the best forms by using the given Elements. I like using outlines, but for this I developed a different solution. I took the Elements and made different variations with different sizes and rotations. After this I began to group these variations and create new shapes. While doing this I realized that the Elements are well chosen: they each have a big potential to create new forms.

After forming the base composition I wanted to create outlines for some of my forms. So, I selected the forms that I wanted to outline and copied them. By pasting these copies with different colours underneath the real forms I achieved the effect that I was looking for.

I used all the Elements in my work because they all have different characteristics. This difference in characteristics keeps the composition dynamic. Major colours of this piece are brown and green and are mostly inspired by colours found in nature. The gradient background is in line with the sunrise theme. Colouring the work was the same as my usual process.

The main challenge was forming the ideas with the given Elements. You must think of all the variations in order to achieve a good result. Sometimes the beauty of composed forms came randomly and unexpectedly. I guess a little bit of luck was needed as well.

Overall I tend to say that the Vormator project actually influenced my design process. When I begin a new project I first try different variations of the elements that I use in a composition. Vormator shows us the power of the Elements and their variations.

Barboleta

designer: Bárbara Emanuel
location: Rio de Janeiro, Brazil
website: www.barbaraemanuel.com

Barbara is a Brazilian graphic designer born and living in Rio de Janeiro – according to her one of the most beautiful cities in the world. In 1996 she started studying Social Communication, focusing on advertising and marketing. After this she continued to study design at Esdi/UERJ in Rio and the Hochschule für Gestaltung in Schwäbisch Gmünd, Germany. Although she has studied a German-orientated school in Brazil and an even more German-orientated school in Germany, colours still play a very important role in her work. She tries to combine the European sense of structure with some tropical flamboyancy; mixing the best of both worlds. Her professional experience includes jobs like graphic designer, art director, design researcher and marketeer.

My work shows the image of a butterfly flying over grass. Transparency was used in the grass layer, in order to accomplish depth and lightness. In the butterfly layer, new forms were created from the Elements mainly through overlapping. By overlapping similar Elements in different tones, it was possible to grasp the somewhat psychedelic feeling of butterflies.

All the Elements were used, so there could be a great multiplicity of shapes and complex detailing. Contrasting with the variety of figures, only four colour swatches were used — three for the butterfly, one for the grass. Each of these swatches was used in different values of tint, therefore accomplishing great colour variation within a very strict palette. After all, butterflies combine extravagant patterns with delicate elegancy.

The piece was designed through different steps. Basic shapes first determined the areas of the wing. Subsequently each one was developed with the careful placement, bit by bit, of the Elements in a more decorative fashion. After the right wing was ready, it was duplicated and horizontally flipped, in order to obtain the exactly similar left wing. The central part was then constructed, joining the wings together. After that, the grass was constructed, through repetition, rotation and scaling of the Wurst Element.

My usual method is to do research, studies, then careful development, and then the most difficult part: recognizing when a piece is ready, and stop messing around with it. So simple, that most people won't do it. As in Alice in Wonderland, when the White Rabbit meets the King:

"The White Rabbit put on his spectacles. 'Where shall I begin, please your Majesty?' he asked.

'Begin at the beginning,' the King said gravely, 'and go on till you come to the end: then stop.'"

The biggest challenge was to create visual flamboyancy from limited elements. Before the Vormator project I worked on a system of pictograms that can be used to design hundreds of icons from a very limited number of elements. Therefore, the system maintains cohesiveness and a minimalist approach to communication. Through the Vormator project, I became even more interested in this kind of construction, where limitations turn out to enhance the design process, providing amazing results.

"Limitations turn out to enhance the design process, providing amazing results."

The Gardener

designer: Baseline
location: Stirling, Scotland
website: www.baselinegraphics.co.uk

BASELINE IS A *small, friendly design company based in the city of Stirling in Scotland. Formed in 2001, the team gets to be creative for many people in a variety of industries. They work with record labels, major music festivals, high street stores, charities and within the public sector doing all the things you would expect a design studio to do across print and the web. Baseline tries to reach a balance of creativity and client satisfaction, and incorporates this into every job they do as well as taking the time to work for themselves on a range of self promotional work.*

Some days you can't decide whether you want to draw ninjas, aliens or robots and other days you draw all three at the same time. This was the result of one of the other days. Making the character a giant pruning a tree was just a side issue that seemed to fit…

I began by building up the leaves using one Element for the leaf, and one for the central vein and using gradients to soften the effect. Then I built up the branches and trunk around it. Once I had a couple of tree shapes, I used the Pathfinder tools in Adobe® Illustrator® to combine the individual Elements so I could repeat and resize them to form the depth and perspective needed to make the forest convincing. The central figure is built in much the same way and a strong, vibrant colour scheme was used to compliment the fantastical nature of the illustration using gradients for a hyper-real effect.

We have always been proud of our chameleon approach to styles, in that our repeat clients often look for different things from different briefs. In order to react to that need, we have to be adaptable. As a result our working methods vary from job to job, using whichever medium we think suits the brief best. Just as Bruce Lee had the "art of fighting without fighting", we've got the "style of no styles"…

For us, the challenge was to try as much as possible to hold true to the principles behind Vormator. Of course there were times we had to divide, crop or use compound Elements to get the right feel, but in the main we wanted to keep the idea to the fore, making it easy for the viewer to pick out the way it was composed and become part of the experiment.

While I don't think that the Vormator Project has influenced my method, it's been a fun experiment and I will more than likely return to the brief again at some point in the future to have another go. It's nice to take a step back once in a while and see how the simplest of shapes can make complex and interesting images.

"We've got the 'Style of no Styles'!"

You're No Fun Anymore

designer: Carlos Andrés Serrano
location: Bogotá, Columbia
website: www.lacapitana.com

Carlos Serrano studied advertising at the University of Botogá and worked as creative- and copywriter for advertising agencies. It was only later that he was given the opportunity to join a multimedia and web design company. This is where he came in close contact with design orientated projects for a wide range of media, both online and offline. Not thrilled by being an employee, he decided to start La Capitana Design Studio together with a friend based in Bogotá. We can tell you that nice things happen over there. Carlos was born in Bogotá, Colombia. He is a lover of huge waves and a true enemy of both broccoli and world domination.

"I see a genuine motivation to say something relevant as the most important part of the design process."

In my illustration an army of wolves has the assignment of taking into indefinite custody all sorts of celebrities from various planets categorized as "not fun anymore" by audience ratings. The illustration is about how we as a human groups tend to idealize people who we then create into monsters and start demanding their heads, when we just don't need them anymore.

I wanted to create expressions and attitudes with the given Elements, by grouping them and adding different scale and rotation values. As you may see, almost all of the components are in solid colour, so I decided to add some depth by using gradients on the sky and the mothership. Two of the Elements went unused and I created a circle by intersecting two Zerks. The circle was used to define a pattern to fill the Droptopus cranial cavity. The colour palette was created to achieve a dramatic effect. To give some 'zombie like' intention to the army, black and white worked just fine.

The process started out one morning while I was watching a news program. I tried to recreate an awkward situation involving a famous local journalist. He thought that the entire country wanted to hear his comments on an event that didn't even take place. He resigned and I knew what my Vormator piece was going to be about. I see a genuine motivation to say something relevant as the most important part of the design process.

There are some similarities between my usual working process and the one used for the Vormator project, in terms of communicating a particular idea through the use of elements present or given by culture or nature and in some cases turning them into new ones that preserve fundamental values and references from the original ones.

My main challenge was to define specific character emotions through the given Elements. It is really nice to see how an intended posture or intention looks, once it has been constructed from Elements that look different from the ones you would normally use.

I really had a lot of fun working on my piece. There are incredible artists involved in the project. For me, the real importance of the project lies in the fact that it joins a group of people from all over the world (or at least what's left of it) around the fact that there are always multiple solutions to a problem. Human beings, despite what's said about them, can create meaningful things from very little.

Smiley

designer: Caspian Ievers
location: London, UK
website: www.smoothfluid.com

CASPIAN IEVERS IS Smoothfluid is Caspian Ievers is Smoothfluid. He regularly points out the difference between a capital i (I) and a lower case L (l). According to him, his best work is still to come. He has worked as freelance designer for companies like Pilsner, Urquel, Nike and Bloomsberry & Co.

HE WORKS CLOSELY to interpret back- or napkin-briefs, liaising with suppliers and developing lasting relationships with all involved in the process. Highlights of his career so far include November & Co's Bochox®, the Counter Culture "Reason for Being" album, various features in ProDesign and Grafik magazines, the design of The Arts Centre's 2006 annual report including a 24 hour behind the scenes photo-docu, and being part of Escea's 600% year 1 growth.

AS WELL AS all this design work he trains new staff in bespoke stationery and typography. His own design company, Smoothfluid, allows him to produce self-initiated projects including a clothing collection. One busy guy huh?

"I don't think there is room for 'normal' in design."

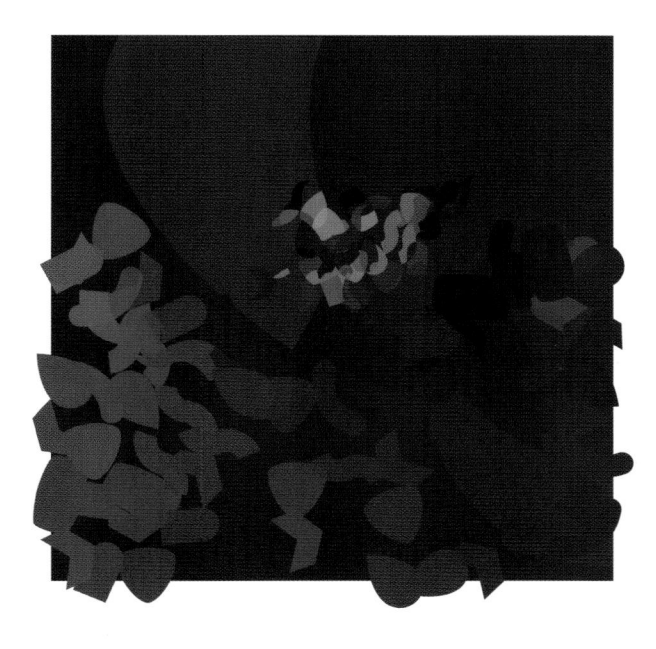

My design is a portrait inspired by Sean Rodwell's fantastic bubble illustrations; finding objects hidden inside scribbles and a cheeky photograph by Sean Warren. A few other techniques were explored before settling on this one, which, despite having a strong digital component, still manages to be alive.

The graphic came to life with a little help from Adobe® Freehand® and Adobe® Illustrator® In Adobe® Freehand® I used the graphic hose loaded with the Elements and in Adobe® Illustrator®, the Pathfinder and Eyedropper tools. Some other useful input came from my understanding of impressionism.

These are the delicate sequences of my usual approach opposed to the Vormator approach:

Usual: brief > ideas > feedback > ideas > feedback > ideas > feedback > bigger logo > happy faces > beer

This time: brief > beer > ideas > beer > happy faces > beer

The greatest challenge was developing a technique that reflected the freedom of traditional media whilst preserving the rigid form of the Elements. Despite this challenge, I have no idea in what way Vormator changed my normal approach to design. I don't think there is room for "normal" in design.

Las Medusas

designer: Christian O'Farrell
location: Buenos Aires, Argentina
website: www.hippiehouse.com.ar

CHRIS IS A *24 year old graphic designer, who completed his studies at UBA University in Buenos Aires. He worked for a year in an advertising agency and he is now seeking new ways of life and expression and delivering illustration as his main means of expression. This is his first published piece, though he has created several urban works. Together with his best friend he is now launching his own design studio, "Hippiehouse", in Palermo, Buenos Aires. They have worked in areas including motion graphics, branding and web development.*

"It's all an act of morphology."

The process was part of a present illustrative intermezzo. I was working on several pieces about the sea and water concept, and with the Vormator project I had the opportunity to generate an abstract piece about this subject. The piece is intended to manifest the underwater magic world with its extravagant forms, colours and animal species such as the illustrated jellyfish, in Spanish called "medusa".

The most common technique used in this piece is transparency, which could be generated with plain or gradient colours. In this case, most of the transparencies were made with gradient colours, to generate the irregular lighting of water under the sea and also to express the different shades of colours. The other important technique was the gathering of Elements to create new forms. This allowed me to communicate and explain this underwater concept much better, generating mainly rounded and organic forms.

The piece was developed with a different working method from the one I usually use. The fact that the rules were clear and precise, the lack of textures and images and because it had to be generated exclusively in Adobe® Illustrator®, changed my way of working and processing. I generally use Adobe® Photoshop® as the finishing platform for my pieces to make the final touches and apply masks, filters and textures if necessary. I took this as the main challenge: having to work in only one design platform with several project rules.

This project has encouraged me to keep on moving, generating things and making me believe in myself. It has also proved that using only five forms, bigger things can be created. In short, it is all an act of morphology.

Pocketful of Posey

designer: Christina Conway
location: San Diego, California, USA
website: www.cconwaydesign.com

Christina Conway is *a San Diego-based freelance graphic designer and illustrator with a habit of creating tactile interpretations of her imagination at play. A former private school art teacher, Conway enjoys working and exploring using a wide variety of media and materials including paper, acrylic paints, ceramic tiles, polymer clay, photography, and anything you can cut, break and glue back together. Current projects through her design company, cConwayDesign, include licensing products, stationery goods, several children's books and using art to benefit community outreach programmes.*

"Rumor has it that the song might really be about the bubonic plague."

Pocketful of Posey is an illustration of four bunny creatures dancing in a ring, surrounded by raindrops and flowers. The title comes from the song that children sing while playing "Ring around the Rosie", which no child really knows the meaning of, only that it is delightful to hold hands, run in a circle, sing a rhyme and flop down on the ground afterward. Rumour has it that the song might really be about the bubonic plague. How delightful indeed!

*"Ring around the Rosie,
a pocketful of posey.
Ashes, ashes,
we all fall down!"*

I loved the challenge of creating an image using limited shapes and I decided to leave the Elements in their most recognizable forms. By cutting into shapes and not deleting anything, the Vormator Elements maintained their simplicity yet congealed, and through transparency lovely new shapes were formed. Out of the eight Elements I was given to work with, I finally used only five. This was not intentional at first but eventually I limited myself in order to cultivate a symmetrical rhythm to the piece.

The colours used for this piece are my standard colour palettes. I adore sweet vibrant colours that remind me of candies and cupcakes. I usually refrain from using a large amount of black, but it helped everything pop and I wanted to create something rather less delicate and innocent than my usual work.

The top centre rabbit creature was the very first thing I made when I initially opened the Vormator Elements file. He was a happy accident of playing around and not trying anything too serious at the start. I wanted to see how breaking up an Element whilst retaining all the pieces would look, as well as alternating colours to keep them recognizable. I thought the character was pretty darn cute and different from my traditional style, so I went with it. As I played with duplicated bunny creatures, positioning them like puzzle pieces next to one another, they began to look as if they were running in a circle. To show individuality I made two very different sets of eyes.

Keeping everything within a square influenced the space I had left to work with. I connected the bunny creatures even more using the ring of orange and yellow raindrops. Everything else came in to play to fill the empty spaces. I often create radiating forms, flowers, snowflakes and suchlike in my personal work, so manipulating the Vormator Elements in this way was a natural choice. And viola! Dancing bunny creatures playing a colourful round of Ring around the Rosie was created.

Ninety percent of my design work is vector based. Therefore, the Vormator project felt very natural, I used Adobe® Illustrator® CS to create every step of my Vormator piece.

Knowing how many talented artists were working on Vormator submissions made it a bit intimidating, but also a wonderful opportunity to showcase my work alongside artists I have come to know and respect – I feel very lucky to be a part of this project. One friend, a design instructor, will even be using this idea for class projects!

Otto Inkwell

designer: Christopher Soprano
location: Bayonne, New Jersey, USA
website: www.portfolios.com/soprano

CHRISTOPHER SOPRANO'S ART *was born out of his instinctive desire to create. As a young child he would make many of his own toys from household objects. It is this ingenuity that is the foundation of his work today. Using imagery from his childhood, Christopher builds visual analogies that are part of his symbolic language. Through a synthesis of intuitive mark-making and calculated visual associations he creates intertwined narratives. This fusing of youthful optimism with cynical doubt makes the work both playful and dark. While revealing clues to their story the somewhat contradictory themes open up the images to multiple interpretations. Familiar subjects become guideposts to ambiguous situations.*

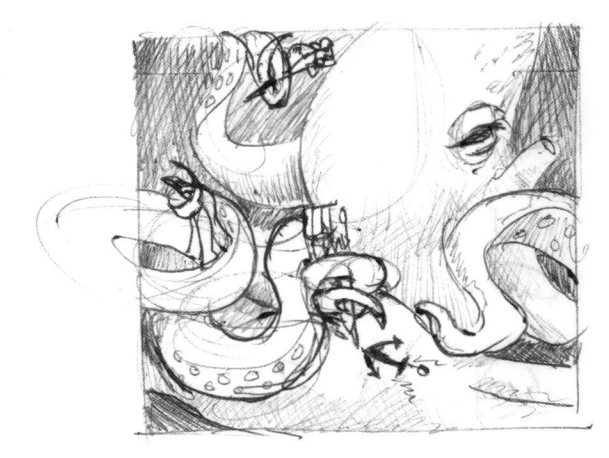

My image stems from my appreciation for tattoo art and my love of the tendrilled form of the octopus. The illustration combines the sailors' myths, which included themes of this sea monster, and their use of tattoos as a visual diary of their journeys. The character is the perfect tattoo artist. He can work four times faster than any human and he can even make his own ink.

Charmed and challenged by the limitless configurations these creatures can take on, I created labyrinths for the viewers' eyes to follow around and through the image. Like an optical rollercoaster, the twisting forms produce a sense of time and depth by moving in and out of the picture plane.

The key to this illusion was overlapping hundreds of Elements. I combined Elements of the same colour in the foreground to create new forms. This method was also used to block some part of the different coloured Elements in the background. This layered effect created the illusion of new Elements. Chromatically, the brighter and larger colours appear in the foreground to create a sense of depth and scale when layered over smaller forms with less contrast.

I began by constructing the tentacles off to the side of the picture to see how many configurations of the different tentacles I could make. Following my pencil sketches I arranged each completed tentacle to match the drawings as closely as possible. The nature of the original Elements limited the range of curves that I could create.

Most of my work is hand-drawn and then altered in Adobe® Illustrator® and Adobe® Photoshop®. Within the parameters of this contest I had to interpret my drawing through the use of the Elements. By eliminating my expressive line work I was forced to focus on the negative space created around the figure. I believe this led me to compose an image with more visual interest.

At first I believed the limitations of the curved Elements would make the image appear too repetitive. My goal was to match the natural curves of my sketches as closely as possible. To stay true to the design rules some tentacles were redesigned using the Elements and other forms, such as the woman getting the anchor tattoo (see preliminary sketch) had to be deleted. I had also set a personal goal to use all of the Elements.

My experience participating in Vormator will help improve how I compose future projects. I have learned that by using a limited number of forms my designs can become more visually homogeneous. I am fascinated by how every piece of art in this challenge was created from the same simple shapes. From the same starting point each artist produced a unique image going in a distinctive direction.

"He can work four times faster than any human and he can even make his own ink!"

You're Free, Now Go For It!

designer: Damian O'Donohue
location: Dublin/Kildare, Republic Of Ireland
website: www.itsdod.com

Damian O'Donohue combines his freelance work with working a couple of days per week in retail. He also does contract work with Réal Design Associates (www.develop.ie). Since graduating from college he has been concentrating mainly on the illustration aspect of Design. Most of Damian's work is character design consisting of the funny, quirky, sinister and sexy. Although pastels and acrylics and other mixed media feature in his work, digital will always have an input. The Vormator Project is the first competition he has entered since finishing college about 5 years ago. So far so good.

> *"He most likely jumped out into the world completely unassisted."*

My illustration displays a very excited new-born baby. I was aiming to portray the sense of sheer joy and exhilaration at being free from restraint (the mother's womb in this case). The umbilical cord is still attached which suggests that he most likely jumped out into the world completely unassisted. This highlights both the urgency we all feel to break free from restrictions and our eagerness to experience new things in life.

I first constructed the composition and layout of the character to see how it would look. This was done using only flat colours as I was determined not to get carried away with cluttering or overcomplicating the image. I never set out to use every Element that was given. I actually ended up using seven of the eight Elements in my design. My decisions on which Elements I would use were based on which ones were more suitable. The Chevron was too sharp and would not blend in with the overall look.

When I was happy with how the Elements were grouped together I added gradients to each of them. This allowed me to blend different Elements together quite seamlessly so that they would not get lost and still remain identifiable to the viewer. The gradients also gave me a lot of freedom when it came to placing objects over one another. His ears, cheeks and hands are good examples of this.

To complete the look I experimented with giving him a shiny appearance all over but that seemed to go against my original goal, which was to keep it simple. His cheeks were the only part of him I kept shiny, which helped draw the viewer's eyes to the face.

I decided from the start that I would use only one Element as the basis for my character, that I would not alter its form and would keep the image clear and simple. I chose the Zerk. Then, in order for me to engage the viewer, I made the same decision for the facial expression: keep it clear and simple. By repeating the same Element for his eyes, nose and mouth it gives the character a well balanced look as well as drawing the viewer's eye. By sticking to these guidelines the character would be immediately recognizable as being created from the Vormator Elements.

My decisions to include his umbilical cord were made for two reasons. Firstly, it added another dimension to the entire image by creating a context for a happy, naked, new-born baby. Without it the character would simply remain static and pointless on the page. Secondly, it showed a simple example of how one Element could be grouped to create a new form.

Subtle gradients enabled me to add a certain depth to the image without over-complicating it.

My final design consideration was whether or not to show the baby fully nude. I am glad it was accepted in the end because it reflects the naughty attitude of the character. My finishing touch was to stick his tongue out.

Normally I work freely between Adobe® Photoshop® and Adobe® Illustrator® to produce various elements in my work. I get to choose whatever I think is suitable for a particular image. This includes textures as well as scanned objects to add depth. So to be restricted by eight specific Elements was a refreshing challenge for me. Every adjustment to the scale, position and colour or gradient that I made was heavily influenced by the rule that we could do as we saw fit, "as long as a viewer of the artwork is able to see that it is composed out of the Elements". As a result I found myself constantly reassessing my design and questioning whether my choices would be acceptable or not.

One thing the Vormator challenge has done for me is to show how effective an image can look without overcomplicating it. Oh, and it has shown that I can deliver on time!

Shogun Invasion

designer: Daniel M. Davis
location: Phoenix, Arizona, USA
website: www.steamcrow.com

Daniel M. Davis is an illustrator and graphic designer. Until he discovered design, he worked as a farm-hand, paint clerk, and baker, doing his own artwork on the side. He has been a professional graphic designer since 1994, which has significantly focused his work. In the last few years he has illustrated, written, and self-published two indie children's books; "Caught Creatures" and "KlawBerry: Good Girl. Bad World." He published under the name "Steam Crow Press" which is run and managed by his wife and himself. He hopes to publish at least one book per year about the other monster world.

Daniel is inspired and influenced by iconic advertising design; specifically advertising mascots found on the wrappers of Japanese candy wrappers, soda cans and cereal boxes. He is also fascinated by toy designs from his childhood, including Jumbo Machinder (Shogun Warrior). Giant plastic robots, monster movies, animation, and vintage objects are also his passions. He currently resides in Phoenix, Arizona with his wife and son, locked in an epic battle against an eternal summer.

My design shows the invasion of an army of giant shogun robots. They are inspired by seventies and eighties robot designs, done in a super-deformed style. I decided to use a very literal rule set for my Vormator piece: no transparencies, no shape manipulations, minimal gradients. Just rotation, scale, and clipping paths using Adobe® Freehand®. I feel that the challenge lies in keeping the shapes as pure and recognizable as possible: if you can use the Pathfinder tool to create any shape that you want, where is the challenge? I only used about half of the Elements. I believe that you really don't need all that many to make something strong and recognizable. I designed Shogun Invasion in black and white, in wireframe mode, until it was almost finished. I wanted a warm colour for the foreground and a cool background, to bring the warriors forward. I have been on a weird purple-pink kick lately, so that just kind of happened.

I started playing with my favourite shapes, working on a few iconic heads, until this design evolved. I love the Tentacle Element, so most of my little icons used that as a primary shape. Once I got the head together, I started adding details like the beard, shadows, and eventually the body. Then I just played with the placement of the body, the scale of the limbs, and the tilt of the head to make it a bit more dynamic. It really came together pretty fast once I decided what the heck I wanted to do.

For me, the big challenge was to make the Vormator project interesting and dynamic. Since I did not develop the shapes myself, I couldn't use my stock techniques to make it flow. I concentrated on some of the foundations of design, like repetition, scale, rotation and colour, since techniques like skew, warp and stretch were outlawed. I think that this concept would make a great challenge for students. In fact, my wife has been using it with her 5th grade class.

Having a very rigid set of rules can be liberating for an artist. Since so much of what we do is problem solving, this sort of exercise is almost easier than "anything goes" assignments since it has some hard boundaries. However, some of the rules turned out to be a little vague; my friend Eric Torres and I debated what the rules meant, and we came up with different conclusions. I think that is probably one of the more interesting things about Vormator: seeing how everyone interpreted the structure of it is really fun. I also find it interesting how one's Vormator piece can look so different from everybody else's, while still looking like one's normal work. I enjoy using Vormator Elements to create simple graphic icons now.

It was a good decision to stay away from shapes like the circle, triangle, and square. The more complex Elements yield a richer array of possibilities. Thanks for inventing Vormator.

> *"My wife has been using this concept with her 5th grade class."*

To Live Again

designer: Daniele de Batté
location: Genova, Italy
website: www.artiva.it

Daniele De Batté *works in various disciplines of visual design. In 2007 he started a project called Take Shape, that creates all sorts of patterns for different applications. It offers a large choice of new and original quality projects. All patterns, whether geometric, naturalistic or symbolic, can be applied to different fields of design including interior design, visual design and fashion. Take Shape designers are inspired by the past, present and future. They create, re-elaborate and invent a fusion of trendy styles in a unique contemporary concept. Despite these vibrant projects, Daniele still works independently as an illustrator and freelance artist. His illustrations are generally black and white, grounded in the world of childhood fantasy.*

THE PIECE UNFOLDS a short story with different characters: The Black Octopus, King Drop, the Lion Man, the Talking Clouds and other mysterious ones who do not appear in the piece. The Lion Man is the most important character because he is the one who creates life. For this work I have used a vector program. I started to play with the available Elements without thinking about a definite subject. At first I placed one Element onto another, creating a new geometry. This process allowed me to continue with my work quickly and provided the opportunity to make changes easily. I have chosen not to use transparencies because I prefer a strong colour contrast; it renders the composition very powerful.

I did not consciously follow a precise scheme but rather a spontaneous progress. Rethinking the process the following phases can be distinguished:

1. analysis of the geometric Elements
2. how the Elements interact (e.g. overlapping and combination of shapes, colour contrast)
3. the creation of characters
4. the set designing

Normally I use traditional techniques such as painting and collage and tools such as ink and pencils. Lately I got hooked to a black BIC® biro, a great tool! Working as an illustrator, I have used digital techniques and vector software. The Vormator project is very close to other work that I have created. I usually start with simple shapes such as rectangles and ellipses and cut and merge these into the final result.

To work with pre-established shapes has been a very interesting challenge. The project has fired my imagination and has reminded me of my childhood when I played with LEGO® putting together odd architectures. In my opinion, this project has been more play than challenge and this is the most important thing!

I would say that this piece is very close to my usual approach to digital works, especially for the use of basic shapes. It has been very useful to understand that restrictions can be more stimulating than total freedom. One can only understand the importance of freedom when there is a barrier to break.

"I would say that this piece is very close to my usual approach to digital works."

Fate Is Great

designer: David Polonia
location: Paris, France
website: www.unstru.com

DAVID POLONIA IS *a Paris-based graphic designer and art director. He grew up in Rodez in the south of France, playing music and learning how to seduce teenagers. He now lives in Paris and works at Publicis Net during the day. At night he is part of a young French collective called You Fuck We Don't that mixes humour, nightlife, and graphic design. His friends Vianney Quecq d'Henripret (Nolenz) and Olivier Bienaimé (Drey) are his partners in crime for this odd project. David loves his job, his boss, his girlfriend, his life, and perhaps even you too. Unstru.com is a digest of all his personal works and feelings.*

THIS COMPOSITION IS a personal interpretation of what life is: Fate cannot be fought. We all come from the same source, the same tree. Throughout life, the leaves we represent follow numerous paths. We experience adventures, happy or not, and we all feel love: the main and the most powerful human sensation. But eventually we all die. So finally, the paths we walk on lead us to death. But for all the experiences we have shared and endured, life deserves to be lived. That is why fate is a great thing.

> "…we, as graphic designers, are accustomed to working with many unconscious habits."

The main shape is centred. The tree was made by placing Drop Elements manually with the help of a circle-shaped guide. Because the heart is an important shape in this piece, I created one by using two Drops. The background pattern was made with a large number of duplications of the same Drop. The change of colours depends on their size. Once the circles were OK, I decided to swap Elements on the z-axis to transform the little circle in the middle to a black tree. This part was duplicated to create a wallpaper for the composition.

South American mythology inspired the colours. The skull at the bottom of the piece is a mix of different Elements, organised to create a terrifying style. The typography is handmade with a manual superimposition of Drops. Although all the Elements were used in this piece, the Drop is the most important.

The Vormator approach to design was very different compared to my usual approach. Normally I start by making a little sketch of the final image I want before even putting my software to work. For Vormator, I did not make any sketch.

The main challenge was simple. I wanted to create something beautiful with the same Elements that anyone else could use, while at the same time trying to preserve what habitually makes your personal style.

Overall I would say that Vormator has not influenced my normal way of designing things. However it was a pretty good exercise for realising that we, as graphic designers, are accustomed to working with many unconscious habits. I think it would make us move fast forward if we tried to escape any of these.

The Bull Rider

designer: David Snider
location: Louisville, Kentucky, USA
website: davidsnider.blogspot.com

David has been involved in design and creative work for most of his life. He was fortunate to have a family full of creative people inspiring him to choose the field of design. He still works for a graphic design firm that primarily designs full coverage graphics for the fleet industry; from small pick up trucks to fifty-three foot lorries. All provide unique challenges and opportunities for exercises in design.

About five years ago things started to change for him with regard to the opportunities that were being offered within the field of design. He found himself getting busier and busier with freelance work and as a result started to operate his own freelance design services under the name David Snider Design Studio.

My piece depicts a lovely bird riding the friendly horns of a bull in a scene set somewhere south of the border. At first, the challenge of creating meaningful art with eight basic and unrelated Elements seemed an impossible task or at best a very frustrating venture. The Elements are just so lifeless and foreign to each other. But I found the challenge to be very enjoyable, bringing life to the once stagnant shapes. After pondering which direction I should take, the idea for my piece just jumped out at me. I set out to take two very contrasting creatures and bring them together in a harmonious setting. Much like the various Elements we were assigned in this project; contrasting shapes brought together to make art.

After establishing the subject and direction in which I wanted to head, I started to study and bring together the Elements that were best suited for the piece. I created a square according to the specs and started to build the art one shape at a time, beginning with the bull and then building out from there, adding the mountainous background and lastly the leafy foreground. Then I came back and added highlights and shadowing to give depth and interest to the piece.

I basically left the shapes untouched, only sizing up and down or rotating them to suit my needs. I tried to avoid creating new shapes from the Elements. I did apply a few gradients to the landscape to provide more distinction to the overall design. I wanted a bright palette of colour to establish the piece geographically. Hopefully the contrasting Elements of Design have come together in a harmonious fashion just like the bird and the bull.

My working method was similar to my normal process of working with vector-based software, though usually I am reproducing design from sketches or reproducing third-party artwork. This was a first for me to take specific shapes to create a new design.

"I wanted it to be appealing to those unaware of the given shapes and somewhat obvious to those involved in the project."

The challenge for me was to create something that was interesting and original, while still maintaining the spirit of the Vormator challenge. I wanted it to be appealing to those unaware of the given shapes and somewhat obvious to those involved in the project that I had indeed used the required Elements.

I don't think I would ever approach a design in this manner. However I feel that exercises like these broaden our designer skills and certainly help us to step out of our comfort zone, ultimately resulting in better design.

Dragon's Battle

designer: DGPH
location: Buenos Aires, Argentina
website: www.dgph.com.ar

"At first we analyzed each Element and tried to find a relationship with the shapes we usually use for our creatures."

Designer Spotlight

DGPH is illustration, is design, is experimentation. In 2005 Martin Lowenstein and Diego Vaisberg decided to follow their own path in the design world with a unique style. Working for different art and design magazines, they created a world of characters and creatures. Their illustrations appear in magazines like IdN (Hong Kong), Fused (UK), Clutter (UK), Belio (Spain), Playtimes (Singapore) and the Pictoplasma Characters Encyclopaedia (Germany). They participated in projects and expositions like Freakypeople (Russia), Design Warriors (Singapore) and Munny Show (USA).

IN 2006 RED Magic Style, a specialized toy company, invited them to create their own designer toy and to customize many others. They entered a new stage, where the characters had volume and substance. Subsequently the studio focused solely on the world of vinyl toys. They are preparing a new 2008 series of vinyl figures commissioned by various international companies.

MOLESTOWN, DGPH'S FIRST illustrations book, is a way to compile some of their works. The visual mixture of different techniques and formats resulted in a new form of illustration that mixes photographs, traditional drawings, digital images and 3D. In 2007 exhibitions were held in galleries like Project, MunkyKing and Blu82 (Los Angeles) and DoublePunch (San Francisco).

THERE IS A big battle with a huge and dangerous dragon surrounded by cute and huggable moles. Because the moles cannot conquer the beast in front of them, they throw lances and nuts. For this piece we tried to preserve the concept and spirit of Vormator. It was our goal to keep a simple and clean illustration, so we did not use any effect or blend except subtle transparency to create shadows. We did create new shapes like the "fish scale" of the dragon. For this we used a Triangle Element in a dark colour, together with the same shape but using the green colour.

At first we analyzed each Element and tried to find a relationship with the shapes we usually use for our creatures. We found quite a few similarities between the two! The only thing we had to create was the story of dragons and moles.

In our daily projects someone in the DGPH crew starts with an illustration or a quick sketch. Usually we start working on paper. This is followed by using the Adobe® Illustrator® software. After that a few Adobe® Photoshop® effects are added if needed. We try to work by hand as well most of the time, but the quality of a vector line is always better than one from our bare hands. So, most of the time, we end up using the digital images.

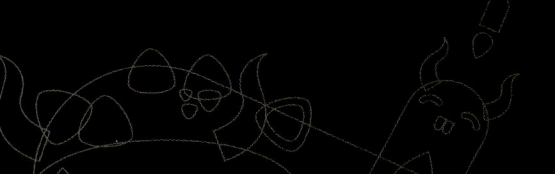

The type of project we enjoy the most is character design. It is the most fun because normally it has something to do with the moles' world that we have already created for ourselves. It is the kind of illustration we do every day. I think it is great when a client gives us a call and asks us to make new characters because of our style and the concepts we use on our guys. I would say that second place is definitely toy design. For us, this is strongly related to character design. Everything we make is supposed to become something else: a toy, a t-shirt, a product for someone to enjoy or just for our own enjoyment. The idea of a design materializing into a product continues to amaze us. I believe it is because of this that we are now trying to create animations with our characters, so that everyone can enjoy the story behind our Molestown.

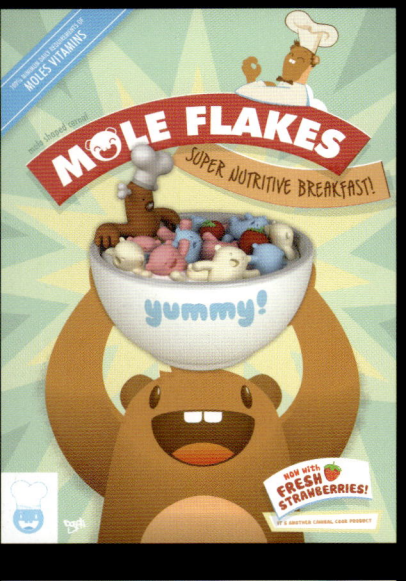

"Everything we make is supposed to become something else..."

Big influences for us are street art, the anime style and old fifties cartoons, such as the Pink Panther or Mr. Magoo, not to mention video games. You can see that reflected in almost every background we make: platforms, gradient in stripes and pixel patterns. We are also influenced by guys like Pete Fowler or Tim Biskup, guys that are doing what they like, creating a mix between art and design in a new way.

The main rule is that we are trying to enjoy our work, as much as we can. We are aiming to work exclusively on illustration projects, art and installation projects, things that we actually care about: toys, music, artists, animation, and to work in the visual field as designers with a different look. We hope that this is reflected in the work we create, where we try to invite the viewer into a new world. A different view on the things people are used to seeing: a more surrealistic and childlike look where dreams are part of the natural things.

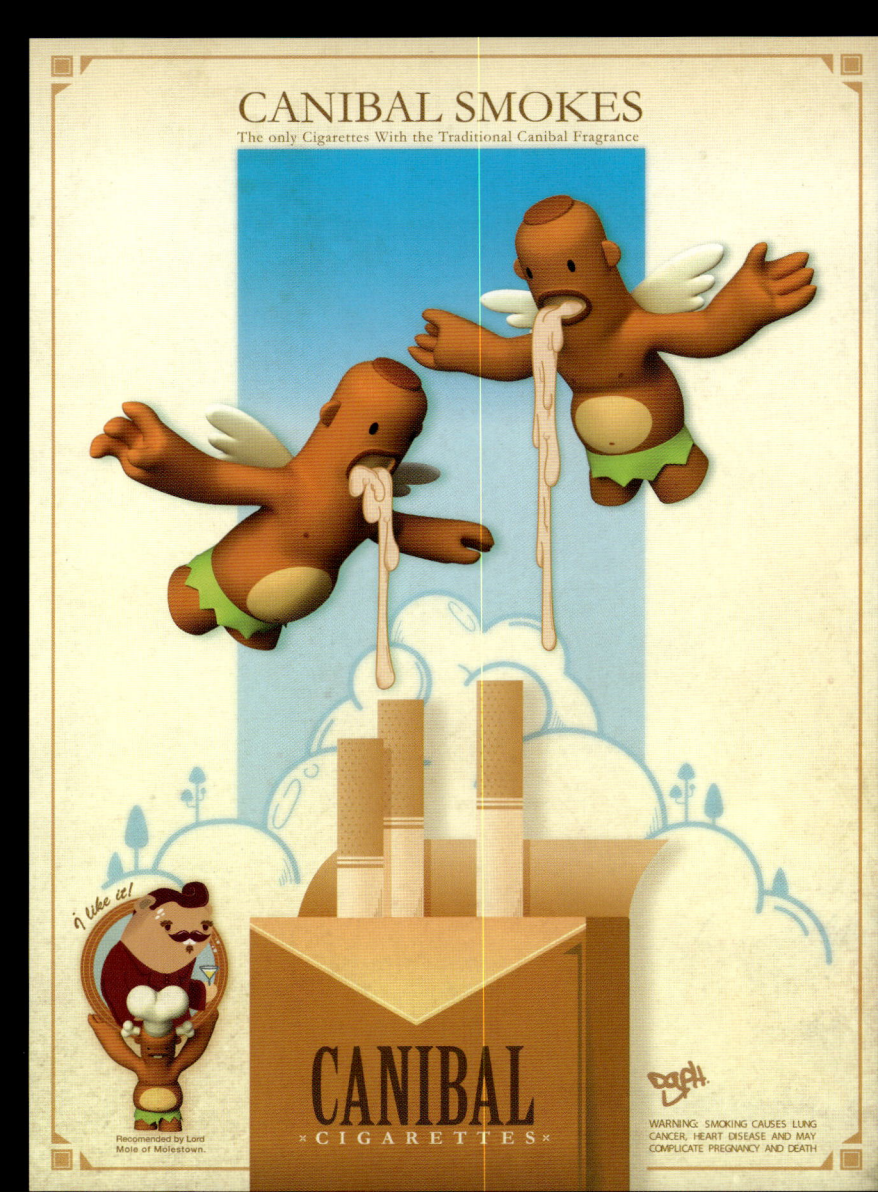

Designer Spotlight

"...everything has the twisted look of both of DGPH heads."

DGPH is formed by three guys: Martin, Diego and Andres. Martin and Diego met each other at the University of Buenos Aires in Argentina. Andres is Diego's little brother, who is studying Industrial Design. Our design studio started as a solution to work without a boss, a way of doing whatever we want when we want, and of course, rejecting those projects that we do not want to do. We started in an advertising agency, but did not even last a year there. Between the three of us, we take care of everything. All the illustrations pass through Diego's and Martin's hands. Maybe this is the reason why our pieces are so weird: everything has the twisted look of both of DGPH heads. Andres spends most of his time rendering everything into 3D characters, animating them and preparing to use them as toys moulds.

Today, DGPH is trying to settle in the globe, offering ourselves as a different solution for traditional things. We are aiming to work more on animation and motion graphics, installations with our stuff and different projects to expand our way of seeing things. A happy way.

The Ritual of the Crazed Imptons

designer: Digart
location: Sydney, Australia
website: www.digart.com.au

BASED IN SYDNEY, Australia, Marc has worked primarily as an illustrator since 2000 under the banner of Digart Graphics. Digart is his 'graphic laboratory' where he breeds all kinds of characters for his illustrations and designs. He draws on a range of influences such as urban street culture, Japanese pop culture, comics, fashion and music that come together in a melting pot of visual ideas.

MARC USES A hybrid of vector and digital imagery mixed with classic analogue drawing techniques, to create imagery that appears anywhere from magazines to billboards, web illustrations, T-shirts and toy-designs.

BESIDES THE ILLUSTRATION work that keeps him fed, other projects he has enjoyed participating in include the Pictoplasma 2 book, Characters at War exhibition, Koa's War of Monsters book, Gaston Caba's Ping-Pong remix project, TDP's Lame Toy character generator, the Tres Logos book and his comic Killcritter City.

To appease the giant green grub queen, the tiny spear-headed 'Imptons' perform a ritual sacrifice as the overhead migration of the 'Star Skaters' begins. As the Imptons pluck their sacrificial prey from the violet night skies, they gleefully dance a jig around the great flower adorned grub. But it is a reluctant queen at the centre of the ceremony, for she yearns to return to her own kind that dwells deep within the grub forest. With every sacrificial mouthful she sheds a small tear drop that goes unnoticed by the whirling, evermore crazed Imptons.

Initially I wanted to keep the shapes quite pure. The small stars in the sky are made up from eight rotated Drop Elements. The wave lines were also repeated in the background to create a subtle pattern in the sky. The city skyline was made up from overlapping various sizes of the Badge Element, then a few darker Badge Elements placed on top to give a bit of depth to the background. The only vignettes are in the tentacles of the creatures flying overhead and the wave lines on which they are floating. The purple, orange, yellow and pink in the colour palette seem to crop up quite a bit in my work lately. I wanted to create a night scene so the purple was the dominant theme. The green for the grub queen seemed to be a

tighter versions of them before moving to the computer, where the majority of the final work is executed. Depending on the job I would scan the roughs in and use my drawings as a template to create the final piece. With the Vormator project I started working directly on the computer because of the specific pre-existing Elements to see what could be created by playing around with the graphic shapes in the vector environment.

When I looked at the eight black and white Elements, I could almost see the shapes as character silhouettes without too much trouble. I thought the characters themselves would develop from the shapes easily enough, so I guess that the main challenge was how they would work in an environment that had to be developed from the same shapes. Because I started out with the characters and then moved on

> *"…the main challenge was how they would work in an environment that had to be developed from the same shapes."*

nice juxtaposition. All eight Elements have been used in the overall design. Seven of the eight Elements have been used just for the creation of the small dancing spearhead characters.

Firstly I wanted to see what characters could be created using the Elements. I knew that would be the preferred direction as opposed to a more abstract design. I played around with the Elements until I had three characters I was happy with. Then I started to play around with the way in which they would work in a composition. At this point I got out the pencils and sketched up various thumbnail ideas of how it might work. In most cases I find it is a lot quicker do some quick pencil sketches to map out where you want to take the design rather than try and design it all directly on the computer. Going back to the computer I then selected a handful of colour swatches to establish a colour palette. Once the composition was set up as per the rough, I could then start to embellish the scene and characters with additional details.

When starting any illustration or design brief I initially consider the ideas and concepts from the brief before picking up a pencil. Then I start with very rough thumbnail pencil sketches, developing

to the composition, (a bit of a reverse way of working), I guess the other challenge was deciding on how the characters would interact with each other. I really like the idea of using a limited shapes palette in the same way you might use a limited colour palette.

A lot of the character designs I create have a simple graphic quality to them. I think limiting a design to just using only geometric shapes pushes that quality even further. I have just created a range of kids' characters where I used my own simple geometric shapes as a starting point and they have worked quite well. So I would say the Vormator project has given another useful dimension to my work process.

The Vormator project has been a challenging and fun exercise in design. It was very interesting to see what could come out of eight little black and white shapes, watching them multiply and morph into the final piece. It was also nice to see something different in the development of the characters that were designed for the piece; it is as if the original elements have given birth to a unique style of their own.

It Is Just a Love War!

designer: Edward van der Veen
location: Utrecht, The Netherlands
website: www.edwardvanderveen.nl

EDWARD IS A young Dutch Digital Media designer currently living in Utrecht, the Netherlands. He recently finished his MA in Digital Media Design at the Utrecht School of the Arts. His design story started in his childhood when he picked up a pencil and began to draw. After a few years Edward wanted to find a way to express his creativity and finally found this in Digital Media design. Furthermore he carries out research in the field of new media and develops concepts for this specific domain. In his concepts he always focuses at the social aspect while keeping an eye on the context. Edward combines digital media design with his passion for graphic design. The playful creative processes of both design disciplines has always fascinated him, and even brought him to London for an exchange course in graphic design.

For Vormator I was inspired by a documentary which I had seen on television about the civil war in Congo. I found it very sad that such a thing is happening in our world, so I asked myself what would happen if bullets contained love. I created a character seated on a giant heart in the sky. This character is bombing the world with so called "love bombs" that have the purpose of making our world a little bit more loving.

I wanted to create a simplistic image so I used the basic Adobe® Illustrator® techniques. I did a lot of research to determine what I could do with the Elements. By combining, overlapping, and scaling I created new shapes. Instead of using the Alignment tool I made groups of the shapes.

Colouring this drawing was a very important process. I wanted to add depth to the composition, so I used gradients and transparencies. The gradients give a shape the illusion of depth and transparencies are used in background elements, such as the white shapes behind the big heart. For the background I have used a brown gradient and the background elements are all white or have a white transparency. The foreground items on the other hand have more intense colours to draw attention.

I started this project by searching the Internet for pictures as inspirational input. Then I started to research the Vormator Elements. I took each Element one by one and tried to create as many shapes as possible using only that Element. After that I did the same thing with more of the Elements. In this way I created a whole set of new shapes which I could use in the final piece. Next, I evaluated the first two steps. The pictures gave me the inspiration for the design. I selected the most interesting new shapes created in my research, and with these I have created the final piece.

Normally I carry out research prior to the generative part. I did the same with this project and divided the project in different research areas. The subject was different from what I normally do; I do not

> *"I took each Element one by one and tried to create as many shapes as possible using only that Element."*

work with shapes in such an intensive manner, because my main focus is concept development instead of design. Studying shapes was new for me in the Vormator project. But I have still worked in my normal structured manner.

I considered the Vormator project to be a huge challenge, pushing my creativity as a designer. I have learned from the project and I believe that my design skills have progressed because I was forced to push my creativity through the limitations. Vormator made me more aware of shapes and composition.

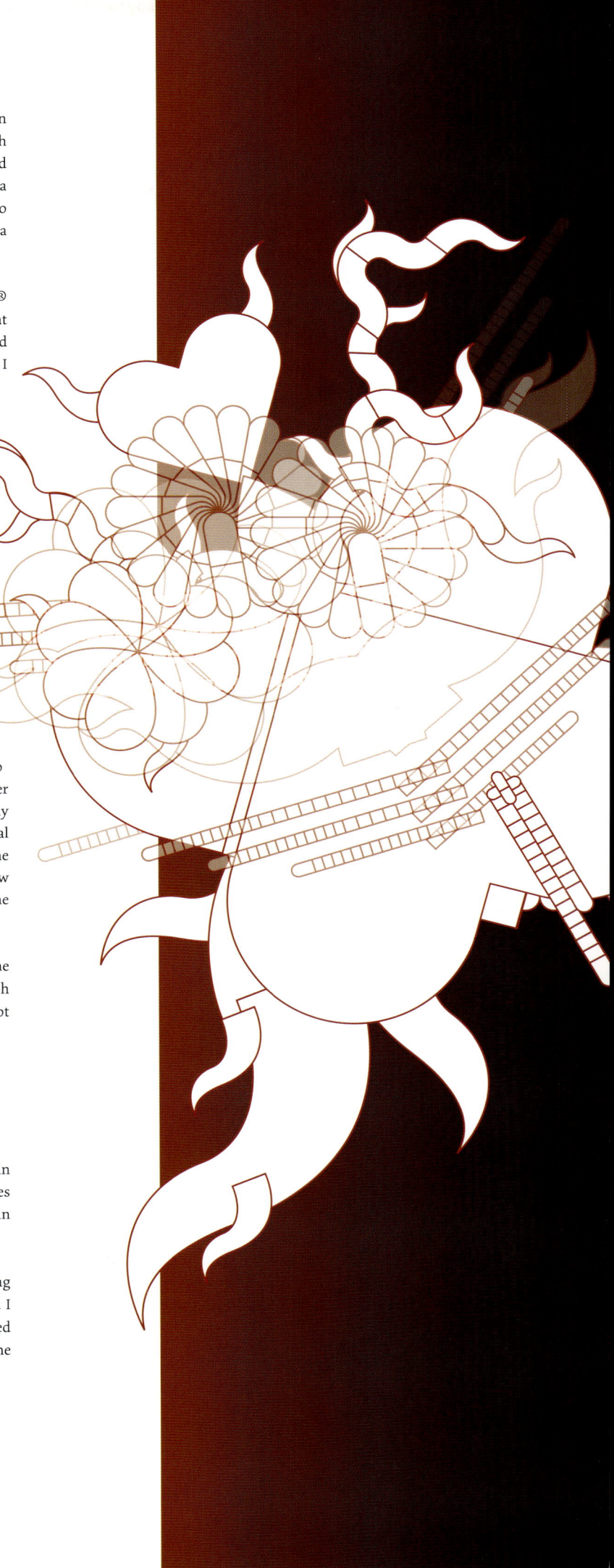

Rules?

designer: El Limbo Von Punsch
location: Paris, France
website: limbopunsch.blogspot.com

El Limbo Von Punsch lives in Paris. He studies Graphic Design and developed his own body of illustrations at the end of 1999. In addition to that he has been listening to and collecting obscure records, making forays into musical composition, and writing in his little black notebook which he uses daily as a verbal and visual diary for drawings and suchlike.

THIS PIECE COULD be perceived as a pseudo-demonstration that contradicts the rules in order to question them – as the naive slogan gives us to understand. Alternately, it could also be an illustrative attempt to create a way to escape these restraints. Anyway you look at it, "rules" is the keyword here…

Each step in the development of this image was an opportunity to use basic shapes in a different sort of way. Basically the idea was to try to use them with thematic layers: abstraction, illustration, typography and pattern.

The first step was to take the size of the Elements and play with them by augmenting them in size to create rather large dimensions within the square frame. This enabled me to evaluate the strength of lines and to display a simple and dynamic background. Next, a parallel work between illustration and typography was developed, where the illustrative parts were composed like a jigsaw. However, the two parts both contained the same "free game", which was used during the manipulation of the Elements.

The whole idea was to have visible letters melting within flourishes or moving as illustrative elements. Also, I wanted to create something futile and to make the rules invisible while at the same time making them the sole subject of the piece. Continuing in the same theme, the pattern work was another expression of the Elements in order to have an additional dimension between the different layers. The last part of the work pertained to the use of colour. The choice of a limited palette of eye-catching colours was intentional in order to keep the maximum visibility of the shapes and

"Basically the idea was to try to use them with thematic layers: abstraction, illustration, typography and pattern."

freshness of the process. Some blending effects have been partially used to create connections between the different layers and to unify the whole.

I cannot say the Vormator project has influenced the way I practice design. For me, restraints and rules are always part of the process in all design projects. This is common where clients and production issues are involved. They do however give the designer further dimensions within the challenge. As a designer one should not just go along with the restraints but creatively absorb them. As I illustrated here, rules can be a starting point and the basis of one's work and the work itself.

This project was a pleasant opportunity to play with rules in a proper sense and to take time journalizing the experience and procedure.

March of the Protectorate

Designer: Eric Torres
Location: Phoenix, Arizona, USA
Website: www.rynaga.com

"I think the ability to create emotion in art and design is a hallmark of the great creative."

Designer Spotlight

Growing up in a big family, in a small town south of Phoenix, Arizona, one might think that creativity would have little room or soil to flourish. However, when drawing is a cheap hobby and time is on your side, one can lay the groundwork for a career as a professional creative with enough practice. That's how things went for Eric anyway. Materially his family did not have much, but he always seemed to have what he needed, including paper and pencils. Drawing was his outlet, his entertainment and his mission. One day he is in high school drawing party flyers, the next he is graphic designer with ten years of experience in the industry.

CURRENTLY, HE WORKS as part of an in-house marketing agency for Arizona's largest financial institutions. His work consists of helping his team to conceptualize and produce successful ad campaigns, branch displays, printed media, and corporate brand initiatives. He and his colleagues enjoy a very creative environment, which leaves Eric sufficiently energized to take on design and illustration projects, both freelance and personal.

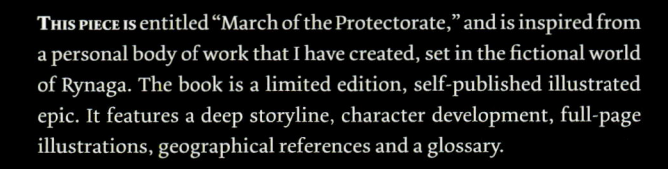

THIS PIECE IS entitled "March of the Protectorate," and is inspired from a personal body of work that I have created, set in the fictional world of Rynaga. The book is a limited edition, self-published illustrated epic. It features a deep storyline, character development, full-page illustrations, geographical references and a glossary.

In this scene, armour clad warriors are marching to what they believe will be their end. They are thinking about the things that warriors throughout the ages have thought of when on the verge of chaos and death – sombre reflections of what their sacrifices really mean, the love of family members, and whether they will survive to see better days.

The technique I adopted with this project focused on overlapping individual Elements to create the illustration. While I spent time experimenting with different forms and compositions, I also thought about the use of colour. In general, I tend to lean towards solutions that make use of a few or several base colours at most. I really like the visual focus that can be communicated by limiting colour choices.

I did not make use of all the Elements when constructing my piece. In fact, I narrowed it down to just five of the eight Elements. In addition, I made use of the Pathfinder tool in Adobe® Illustrator® to achieve some hybrid shapes derived from the originals by intersecting, dividing and merging shapes. In the end this kept most of the lines in my submission curved, which I think helps to create an organic aura.

I like to start at the thumbnail stage when developing a piece of art or design. Drawing and quickly transposing thoughts and mental images to paper is key to extracting the most value out of the creative process. So, I usually start with thumbnails that address general composition and grid patterns. Then I will give thought as to how I might break up the grids to create interesting layers and perspectives.

Having let some of that initial creative energy out by sketching and drawing, I next turn to research, data gathering, and the logistics of the project. Depending on the piece I am working on, there can be a whole host of concerns that need to be addressed. Target audiences, media types, production guidelines, budgets, and so much more can influence creativity. What is important is learning to be inventive while working within constraints, rules, and pre-determined conditions.

I then try to give thought to the mood of a piece and how I might capture that mood visually. I think the ability to create emotion in art and design is a hallmark of the great creative. From writers and musicians to painters and theatre performers, it seems as though creating an emotional response in your audience is the common "golden thread" in artistic expression. This is something I am working hard to improve in my own artwork.

The Vormator project took me on a journey outside of my comfort zone, challenging me to focus on different avenues to creative problem-solving. This project has greatly influenced the way I see my art and has even terraformed the landscape of my own imagination to a certain extent. Now, I tend to see geometric images not just for what they are, but what they could be.

The main challenge for me with this project was really just deciding what to illustrate. I had several ideas and most seemed to offer some good potential. However, I chose to create an illustration for a written body of work that I already had, something that had already saturated my creative thought patterns. In the process, that project was taken to a whole new level of creativity. What amazes me now is how one challenge like the Vormator project can greatly inspire the imagination.

"My passion is to inspire my audience to think more about creating art, rather than just consuming it."

Designer Spotlight

Normally I start at the drawing board, quite literally. I doodle, make a word map, brainstorm connecting ideas and make lists. Keeping notebooks is also an important part of the design process for me. My tools include Adobe® CS, a Wacom® tablet, sketchbooks and lots of whiteboard space. I really try to start the design process outside of the computer realm first. Then, once I think that I have a good understanding of the objectives and main purpose of a project, I begin using the computer as a tool for influencing the creative solution.

Much of my daily work consists of design for in-house agencies. For example, I had the opportunity to produce pieces for UPS, Toyota and Bristol-Myers Squibb. More recently, I have had the privilege of helping a local financial institution here in Phoenix further its brand presence as part of an in-house marketing team.

Vormator has influenced my design and imagination in many different ways. Currently, I am developing the "World of Rynaga" (rynaga.com) – a complete world-building exercise that includes an original epic storyline, historical data, character design, music and illustration. I am proud to say that I have taken the principles and Elements of the Vormator project and applied them to my first book about this world, entitled "Prelude". This work is devoted to exploring the use of limited shapes to create the visuals for a fictional world. As other pieces of the story are told, I plan to use the same rules that applied to the Vormator contest, but with new shapes or elements.

Some of the most influential artists in my life are Genndy Tartakovsky, Peter Chung, James Jean, Sanna Annuka, Klaus Haapaniemi and Erté. I am most inspired when I see other artists incorporate drama, emotion and storytelling in their work—ideas I strive to capture in my own body of work as well.

My passion is to inspire my audience to think more about creating art, rather than just consuming it. By being a creator, as well as a consumer, I think people can achieve more self-esteem and satisfaction in their careers and perhaps in life in general.

Growing up, I drew and read as much as I could about art and art history. Over time, I developed an eye for graphic design, use of type and composition. It wasn't until several years after I graduated from high school that I was able to achieve my degree in Visual Communication. For me, success in the design industry has sprung from a mixture of hard work, presenting myself and my work professionally, and understanding business objectives. It is also vitally important that I continue to study design, read constantly, and create artwork and products that reflect my creative vision.

Kaleidoskull

designer: Erik Varusio
location: Vicenza, Italy
website: www.erikvarusio.com

Erik graduated from the Venice Academy of Arts. After years spending his time drawing and painting he finally acquired his first computer. And it has been a love story ever since. In 2006 he finally got his first fulltime job as designer, happy to breathe design on a daily base.

Erik is fascinated by the infinite possibilities of the digital medium. To him it provides the opportunity to mix different images and styles. He is convinced that the strongest designs are the ones in which the elements create an ensemble where every piece is necessary in its particular world.

"My main challenge was to obtain sort of a spatial depth with two-dimensional geometric forms."

For this piece, a crying/smiling skull face, I have used five Elements. The use of transparencies and gradients enabled me to play with a tri-dimensional effect. Opposing and overlapping the Elements creates different shapes.

I started building the face: the Badge for the head shape and for the nose, the Bar in the place of the jaw, several Drops as eyes, two Wurst Elements as arched eyebrows and some Zerk Elements as teeth. Once the main skull-element was done, I repeated it twice: the first time rotated by 180°, then one in the original position, thus creating 3 main layers. Playing with the transparency and layer effects again, I obtained the 3D-Kaleidoscope effect.

For this piece I first tried to make a selection of the Elements that would enable me to build the particular world. Having no theme-purpose I began by just letting my eye-hand-brain play with the Elements. After some natural selection I focused on this 3D-repetition effect made with simple, flat shapes.

My main challenge was to obtain sort of a spatial depth with two-dimensional geometric forms. I tried to do that as simply as possible to give it harmony and to let the observer's eyes eventually discover the single blocks of this LEGO® like sculpture.

I must admit that every single image that I make influences the way I normally design. I love to solve different problems in every new project. It was great fun to use a set of pre-defined Elements and use them in an unexpected way.

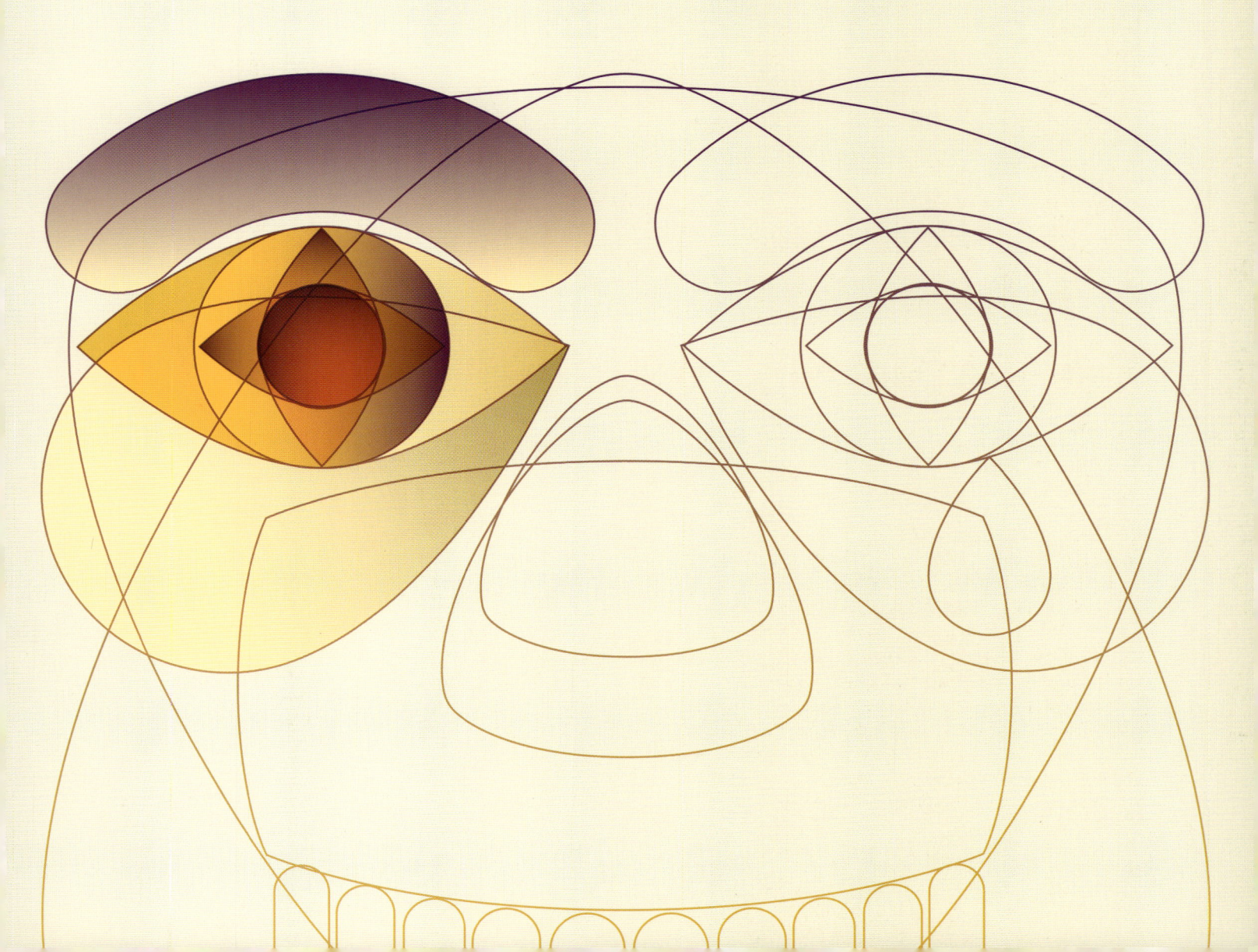

Don't Eat That

designer: Fredrick Aven
location: London, UK
website: www.unit9.com

Born in a small rural town in Sweden, Frederick always found it interesting to illustrate. Not so much because of his skills, but because of the lack of anything else to do. Mix this with his love for fluffy animals, vectors and panda-dogs and it is obvious where he's heading.

At the age of 19 Frederick moved to the UK to get a BA (Hons) at the Cumbria Institute of Arts. It gave him a great chance to develop a lot of techniques and to learn about composition. At first he was fixated on the print business. But after getting an internship at Unit9 in London, that quickly changed and he came to love animation and Adobe® Flash®. Now he titles himself an interactive designer at Unit9, learning to animate like there's no tomorrow and drawing lots of monsters.

> **"The first breakthrough I had was when I realized how I could do a circle."**

It was the original idea to create a well-composed illustration in which everything is contained in this circle of chaos. Initially I thought the genie in a bottle myth could be a good start but halfway through I decided that this concept was rather limiting. So out went the genie and in came a lot of monsters, creating more of a visual representation of imminent food poisoning awaiting you under that shiny silver lid.

I started off with the idea that I wanted to do a circle where a lot of characters are contained and interacting with each other. After that I came up with a couple of different settings where this could take place, but decided in the end that a food platter with a bunch of evil and misunderstood monsters would be the most rewarding route for me to take.

This project was very much an exercise in adding and dividing objects until I achieved the organic feeling I wanted. No transparencies were used, but instead I used the different Pathfinder tools in Adobe® Illustrator® to create solid shadows. This was also how most of the shapes in the image were created. I didn't really limit myself to one kind of Element but used the ones I felt were appropriate. Saying that, you can see that there are some recurring shapes that I used throughout.

I wanted to keep the focus on the circle of monsters and decided to give them all pretty vibrant colours. This was to give it some more life but also to give me a bit of a challenge seeing as how I am usually very sparse with my colour use. I then sat down to experiment with the Elements we were given, trying to come up with as many organic shapes as possible whilst still trying to keep the characteristics of the Elements. The first breakthrough I had was when I realized how I could do a circle, not much of a breakthrough really but it was significant for the rest of the project.

This project did not differ that much from my usual workflow. I have a love for vectors and I have always been prone to create very basic characters, making the most out of the shapes. I early on decided that I wanted to have as much colour as the concept allowed without losing the style. I usually work with three to four colours in my palette but found it very refreshing to use such a wide variety of colours and still create a successful composition.

I think the hardest part of this brief was to interpret it; to realize your limitations and discover that they are not really limitations if you just put enough work into it. I could have created anything with this brief. It is just a matter of being clever about it and exploring how objects can be combined to create any shape at all.

Missensate

designer: George Tsolpakis
location: London, UK
website: www.georgetsolpakis.co.uk

GEORGE TSOLPAKIS WAS *born in Thessaloniki, Greece, in 1978. He has been actively practising graphic design for commercial and non-commercial purposes for the last eight years. Having extensively studied many aspects of the discipline in various European cities including Berlin and London, he has gained a deep visual knowledge and developed an eye for detail. His latest endeavour to master design was an MA course in which he explored in depth conceptual, visual and theoretical typography. Currently he is engaged in freelance design while developing his personal ideas and projects.*

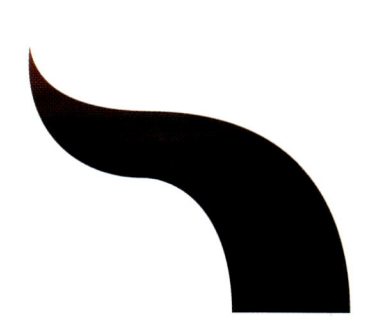

Not that rare: when we look upon an image a sense of smell or touch is triggered. The same thing occurs sometimes with all the senses. "Missensate" is a made-up verb for describing this particular action of the brain, the mis-triggering of the senses, and accordingly the visual is meant to do exactly that. Presented to thirty individuals, more than two thirds have experienced a vague feeling of touch, almost like a distant memory of a surface that they (including myself) felt when they were young.

The process of creating the piece was relatively simple. Only one of the eight Elements is used, repeated continuously throughout the page in order to give the feeling of a mass or surface. After applying a red to black gradient on the element that blended in partially with the background colour, I placed it in the top left corner of the page. Then by copying and pasting the Element, overlapping the first Element, and by repeating this process, I created the first line. After grouping this first line, I duplicated it and placed it a bit lower with the alignment being slightly off. I repeated this process until I reached the bottom of the page thus creating a surface-like mass that seems slightly elevated. When the page was completely full I went around the edge of the artwork, selecting each shape individually, and using the Pathfinder tool, getting rid of the part that was bleeding off the page. Then, using the gradient tool, I adjusted the angle and the position of the blend in order to bring it back to its original effect.

> *"Knowing when you reach the stage where you have to stop developing can be tricky."*

After studying all the Elements individually and after brainstorming, I came up with an idea, which was to create a non-realistic visual that would remind us vaguely of something we all came across at some point in our lives. Something with a slight resemblance to the real world. Immediately after, I started researching how humans perceive images. I began to reduce my surroundings to geometric shapes and then looked for a resemblance between the Elements and the real world. When you want to find such a resemblance, reducing real life to geometric shapes is really important since our brain registers everything in shapes. Researching was probably the most important stage, since the whole piece would have been meaningless without a solid background. Only when the preliminary stages were complete and I could finally visualise the idea I started to create the piece.

I call my process BRC: Brainstorm – Research – Create. These are the key stages of my (and I'd like to believe every designer's) usual working method. The design process is an evolutionary technique where the visuals and concepts shift, change and adapt while the project is growing. The only difference with this project was the starting point. Being given the Elements beforehand, they had to be studied before anything else could happen. That in itself was both helpful and restricting.

The main challenge in creating the piece was knowing when to stop changing and developing it. As this is an ongoing and endless process with the only limitation being time, knowing when you reached the stage where you have to stop developing can be tricky.

Due to this project and the research I carried out for it, my perception of the real world's visual stimulation has somewhat changed. Since finishing the piece I am more prone to reduce my visual reality to shapes and then look for patterns and repetitions which can be applied to the design process. Overall this has given a fresh breath of air to my design technique that can be seen in my latest projects.

Vormator Typeface

designer: Glasfurd & Walker
location: Vancouver, Canada
website: www.glasfurdandwalker.com

"The challenge was to create a consistent, unique and uniform typeface out of somewhat awkward shapes."

Designer Spotlight

Phoebe Glasfurd is an Australian Designer. Graduating with a Bachelor of Arts in Design from Curtin University (Perth) and Honours in Communication Design from Swinburne's National School of Design (Melbourne), Phoebe moved to Sydney to take up the position of designer at Ink Project. During her time there Phoebe worked on small and large-scale print and broadcast branding projects, for both local and international clients. In those three years, Phoebe's design work won numerous international design awards.

MORE RECENTLY PHOEBE has moved to Vancouver and set up Glasfurd & Walker with producer Aren Fieldwalker. Glasfurd & Walker is a design studio which focuses on a range of moving image and print projects. With careers crossing print and moving image design, branding, live action and post production, they collectively explore areas of design they know and love, as well as new areas such as textiles, fashion and product design.

ON SEEING THE challenge Vormator proposed we wanted to create a piece that served a function beyond the purely aesthetic. We had been searching for a concept for a new typeface and thought the Vormator submission was a great opportunity. The Elements presented the challenge of creating letterforms from unique and seemingly unrelated shapes by formulating a logic intrinsic to their relationship with one another.

Using the eight Elements we have built patterns and shapes by adhering to a grid and a formula that used the shapes in their purest form – taking this as the most important part of the brief. We did not use transparencies, blends or other techniques to get more out the Elements. We simply played with pattern, composition and structure to create the required shapes, angles and curves needed to create the typeface.

The following steps were taken in creating this design: First, I developed a palette of patterns/shapes to make up the typeface, then created a grid for the typeface to adhere to and then started using the shapes to construct each letter. When this was ready I started to explore colour application to the typeface. The final submission assigned a specific colour to each shape. It was interesting to see the distribution of the shapes throughout the composition.

The working order of concept, development, design and refinement is a fairly standard process for me. However, the nature of the execution was something reserved for process of typeface creation. The challenge was to create a consistent, unique and uniform typeface out of somewhat awkward shapes. It was an interesting exercise, being dictated all the content of the design and having to create something unique from it.

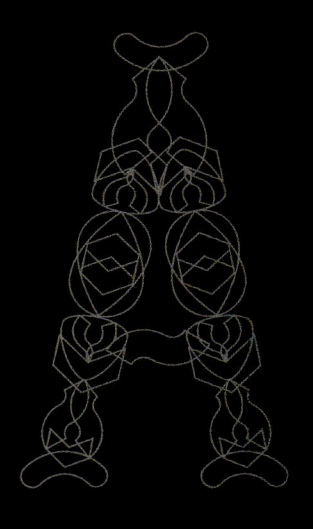

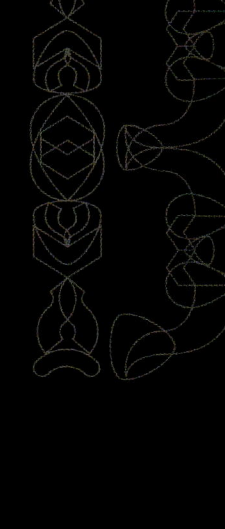

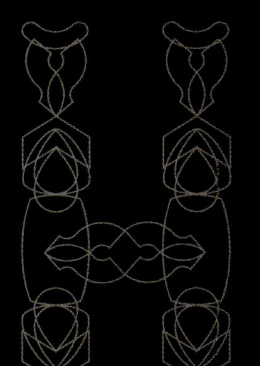

GLASFURD & WALKER

"...the fine balance between the artist and the reality of the commercialized world we live in."

CAPPUCCINO 2.50
FRENCH PRESS COFFEE 1.75 **latte 2.75**
MACCHIATO 2.25
ESPRESSO 1.75
AMERICANO 1.75 *Hot Chocolate 2.75* **LOOSE LEAF TEA 2.25**
MOCHA 3.25
EXTRA SHOT, FLAVOUR, OR SOY 0.50

In my usual work, most design starts with some research, either for inspiration or reference depending on how specific a brief is. Like any designer I have collected a lot of inspirational material, as well as a reference library to call on if needed. From there the conceptual and design stages can entail illustration, photography or pure graphic design, it all depends on the brief and best execution to answer that. Adobe® Illustrator®, InDesign® and Photoshop® are my preferred software.

I tend to work on a fairly diverse range of projects for a variety of clients. The scope of creativity is much broader and I enjoy the challenge of diversity. At the moment the studio is working with clients in product and fashion design, non-profit and environmental, corporate, travel & lifestyle and the arts. For most projects that I work on, I act as creative/art director, designer, illustrator and finishing artist. At the moment I am brushing up on my photography skills. I love vector-based illustration, but also find inspiration in photographic and moving image. I think my style is still developing, so it is hard to define it right now. My influences change on a daily basis, depending on the project I am working on.

Designer Spotlight

bg
BRAGDON GLOBAL GOODS

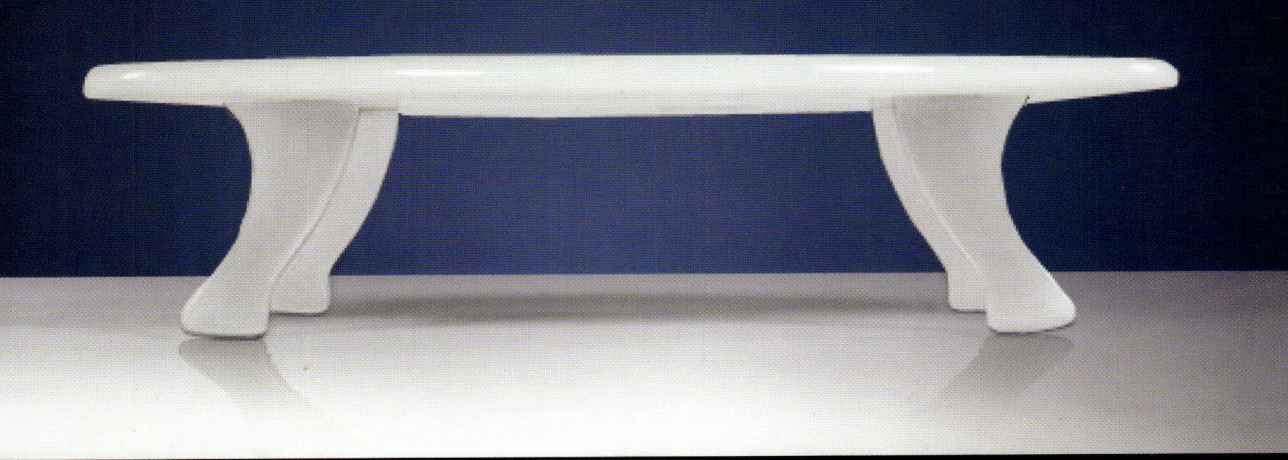

The end goal really does depend on the project. Sometimes I just aim to satisfy my own taste, sometimes I try to answer a very specific brief, sometimes it is a mix of the two. I suppose it is the tight rope every designer walks... the fine balance between the artist and the reality of the commercialized world we live in.

After four years working in the industry across print and broadcast design, I opened my own studio for the same reason most people do: to be in control of my own creativity and have the ability to explore new areas of design.

the PAINTED BIRDS

The Sea Monster

designer: **Gorky**
location: **Milan, Italy**
website: **www.gorky.it**

LUCA ARRIGONI IS *a graphic designer living and working in Milan. He studied visual communication at the Politecnico University of Milan, where he practiced with typography and illustration. He loves taking part in graphic contests because they are a good opportunity to compete with other artists, to grow and improve his skills. He told us that working as a graphic designer takes a lot of patience. It is not even unusual for him to work at night to create and finish original works. In the end, when Luca looks at his finished piece, he wants to feel satisfied.*

"There's no fear of handling the blank page because you already have all the ingredients."

The Sea Monster is in everybody's mind. Movies, books, legends... After all, who has never in his childhood fancied close encounters with black, huge, tentacled creatures, ready to crunch or crush unlucky boats crossing their way?

At first I played with the basic Elements for a long time, trying to understand what kind of combinations were possible. I was duplicating, rotating and flipping them without using the scale tool. In this way I have extended the start Elements kit, adding new coordinated shapes by using the drawing tools, and so developing multiple choices.

Once I fixed the project subject I tried to find the perfect match between the shapes and my abstract idea whilst discarding the unhelpful shapes. Then I created the main character and the typography. This helped to achieve the same style as the first-stage Elements, and to build the sea scenery. I used gradients for the background to give more depth and to simulate the effect of the volumetric light on the surfaces. I also used transparencies applied differently on the group of jellyfish mixed with the radial gradient (from green to yellow) to simulate the creatures' texture. Finally I added shadows under the stones and the pink monster to give more realistic details. The result is a mixed work of 2D and 3D features.

For me, playing with predefined Elements is a more exciting process and a simpler working method than creating brand new shapes. There's no fear of handling the blank page because you already have all the ingredients. It is more an issue of editing, and an activity that resembles playing Tangram® and looking at the sky to see what clouds look like. I can almost say that using this kind of approach, the artwork developed itself.

The main challenge was to force myself to follow an extra rule: I tried to add shapes, without subtracting or intersecting them, to avoid making the original Elements unrecognizable. This made me feel that I could get an output in line with the Vormator philosophy.

Typographic design was the hardest part of the entire project. To obtain congruence between different letters, I only used the Tentacle Element to design the entire character set. In my view boundaries are helpful and encourage the creativity to outsmart them. The Vormator project was an opportunity to play with these limitations. I also think that limitations are always present in regular work, imposed by clients and their crazy requests. The secret of making something is doing it with pleasure!

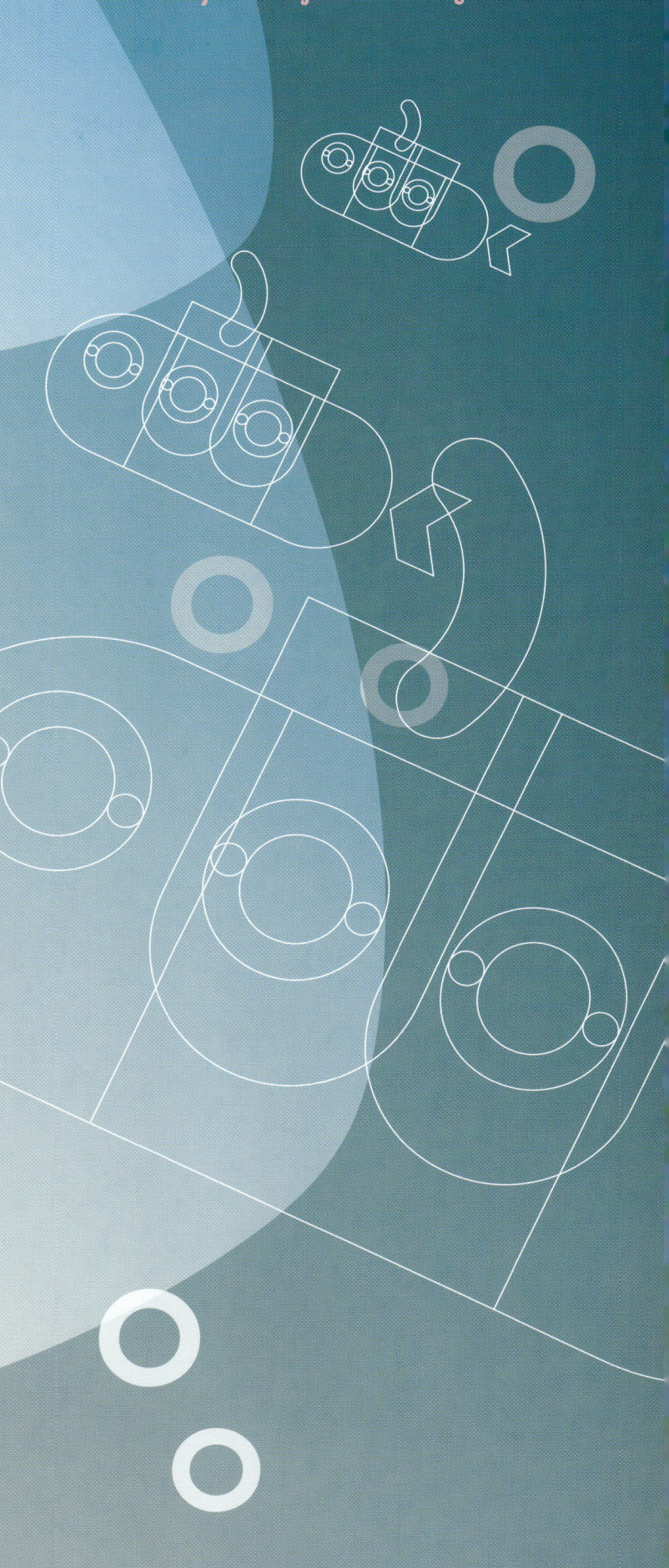

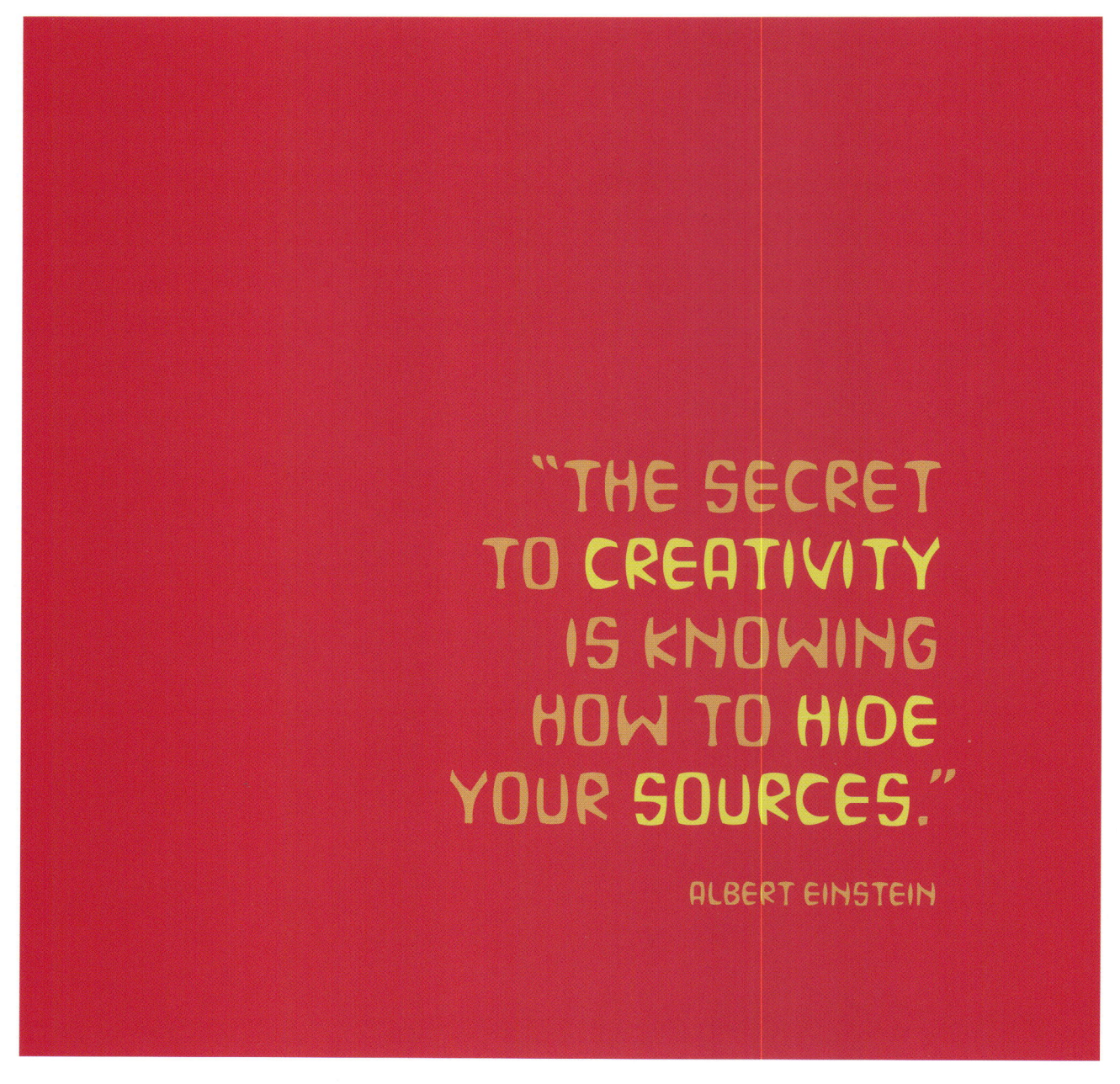

"THE SECRET
TO CREATIVITY
IS KNOWING
HOW TO HIDE
YOUR SOURCES."

ALBERT EINSTEIN

Vormator Typeface

designer: Grootfontein
location: Paris, France
website: themeteorite.blogspot.com

GROOTFONTEIN IS A French graphic designer and illustrator who lives in Paris with his wonderful wife and his adorable silly son. He eats chocolate everyday because it is good for him. For the same reason he draws something daily. He works for children and adults in both publishing and press, though his true passion lies with animation. Because he usually works directly on the computer, he tries to give his images a friendly handmade feel by adding scanned textures. He likes to play with chance in his work, so he developed a random technique that allows him to create fun illustrations. His style is much influenced by the animation styles of the fifties and sixties (like UPA® cartoons), as well as Saul Bass' work.

My Vormator piece is a font constructed from all the eight Elements of the Vormator contest. It was my basic idea that the original Elements needed to be recognizable within each letter. So each glyph had to be very simple.

I chose to design the individual letters using the negative shape drawing because this is not the obvious approach when creating a font. Each letter is based on one, or a combination of two basic Element(s), from which I subtracted a few other Elements (up to five). For example, the general silhouette of the "G" is composed of the Bar Element. Then I subtracted the Chevron and the Badge to give the "G" its final design. The most difficult part was actually to design the numbers and the punctuation glyphs. I spent a lot more time on the numbers and punctuation glyphs than on the letters.

In my opinion, the first (and most important) step in the design process is to find the idea, style or universe. For Vormator I told myself: "There will be hundreds of graphic submissions; I have to find a way to be different…" So I designed a font, reasoning that a typeface would probably be more original than one of my illustrations. The second step was to find a design principle, in my case the negative shapes. When the design principle was determined, I began to build the letters. I always kept an eye on the homogeneity of the glyphs. The last steps were to test the font in some random text and to make the final adjustments (kerning, shapes balance, leading).

> *"My real Challenge though was to complete the design of the twenty-six letters during the nap of my two-year old son."*

It was one of my challenges to build readable glyphs under the imposed restrictions while proposing a fun and pleasant font that could be used in other graphic works. My real challenge though was to complete the design of the twenty-six letters during the nap of my two-year old son. Luckily, he napped for three hours that day!

I am used to working with constraints like colours, size, readability and time. Often I find these constraints stimulating for creativity. Yet working with only eight Elements as constraints was quite something. Because I chose to design a typeface the project did more than influence the way I normally work. It has given me a new range of opportunities!

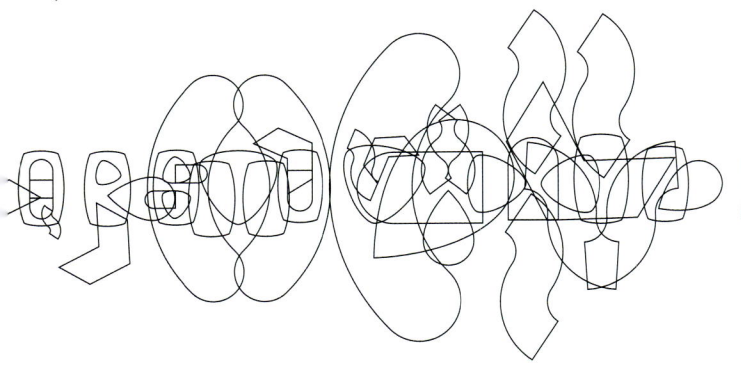

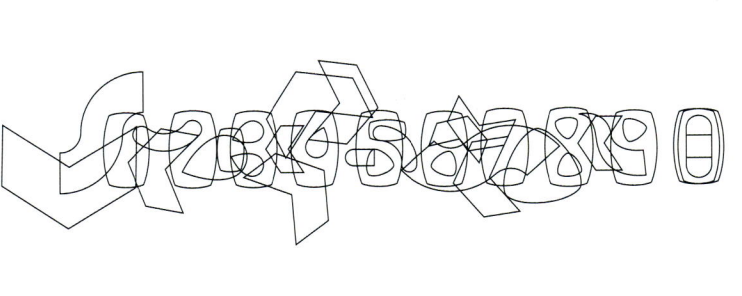

Missing: Heart, Brain, Courage and One Small Yappy Dog

designer: Hilary Leung
location: Toronto, Canada
website: www.s4le.com

Hilary Leung is *a designer by day and illustrator by night. Having spent the last five years pursuing other dreams, he is happy to return to his first true love: drawing. His design work can be found hot stamped onto his other obsession, ultimate frisbee. His rotating ambigram disc designs can be found soaring through the skies worldwide. The Vormator project was right up his alley, as he loves the excitement of solving puzzles and design problems.*

THIS ILLUSTRATION IS based on characters from L. Frank Baum's "The Wonderful Wizard of Oz". I was seeking to capture the moment Dorothy and friends met the Wicked Witch of the West and her team of Flying Monkeys and I imagined that the quartet was not amused. Hopefully this aerial snapshot of the Lion, Tin man, Scarecrow and Dorothy drives that point home.

The eight Vormator shapes provided were very generous, so it was my intent to keep the Elements as pure as possible. Transparency allowed me to create new forms while still maintaining the integrity of the original Elements. This technique was used in the Lion's mane, Dorothy's dress and Scarecrow's collar. Grouping Elements made it easier to move or transform my characters independently from everything else. Blending was used in the shadows to elevate the heroes from the background. I used all the Vormator pieces except for the Cobra. I don't like cobras.

"Starting in black and white allowed me to appreciate the potential inside the positive and negative shapes."

The very first step I took was to create a grid. I then scaled down all the Elements, so that they would fit into the grid. Next came the fun part: I played, moved, connected, rotated, mixed and matched all the Elements together. Some interesting shapes I explored included the chain, wave, donut and various flower patterns (much like the Spirograph™ toy from my childhood). Starting in black and white allowed me to appreciate the potential inside the positive and negative shapes. Simplifying was the trickiest part in this challenge. It was really easy to complicate the piece with more shapes and patterns, but I needed the original Elements to shine.

After developing these delightful patterns, I thought about how I could apply them to an illustration. The Lion's mane came first, then Dorothy's dress. Everything quickly fell together. It made sense to use a bird's eye view. Originally I thought about dropping the Witch's shadow over the heroes. This caused unnecessary clutter and it obscured the simplicity of the piece. Plus, I thought it would be more fun for the viewer to discover the Witch's point of view.

Seeing as how this was a children's story, it was natural to select a vibrant colour palette. The yellow brick road was tinted green to contrast the yellow Lion. I used the Adobe® Illustrator® Pathfinder tool to divide the overlapping pieces in the Lion's mane. This allowed me to manually increase the contrast, thus control the way it appears.

The primary objective in most projects is to solve problems using time and money as efficiently as possible. The primary objective for the Vormator project was to have fun. This was a personal voluntary exercise with no pressure to create a masterpiece. I really cut loose and had a lot of fun. The Vormator project has indeed changed the way I design. I am much more limber having stretched my creative muscles. Vormator has re-awoken my dream to publish my own line of children's books.

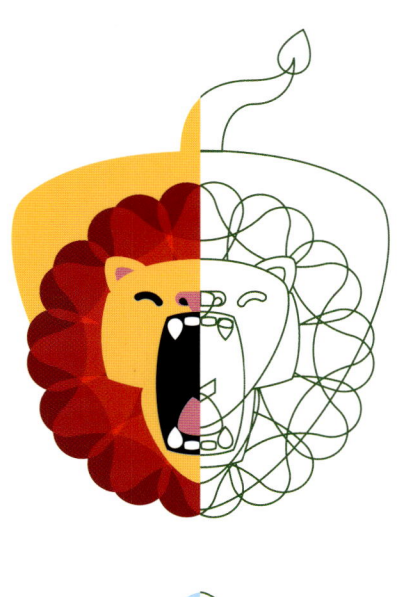

Kendra's Present

designer: **Hui Chin Heng**
location: **Johor, Malaysia**
website: unknown

HUI CHIN HENG *studied at The One Academy of Communication Design, Malaysia, and received his degree in Advertising & Graphic Design. Currently he works at AE models, a model and exhibition booth design company. This job taught him many skills as well as graphic design, including exhibition booth design. As a fresh – though not naive – graphic designer from Malaysia, he is still seeking that silver lining between commercialism and design. Hui loves travelling and lomography and believes in the wonders of communication through design, especially in this world where everyone belongs to a certain race, and speaks a certain language.*

This idea was born when I wanted a piece of wrapping paper for a friends' birthday gift. I wanted wrapping paper that would tell a story about my gift, so together with three other friends we bought four gifts because it was my friend's twenty-second birthday (2+2=4, get it?). Eventually, with the Vormator Elements incorporated, it turned out very interesting indeed. We packed our 4 gifts together, and I think she loved it!

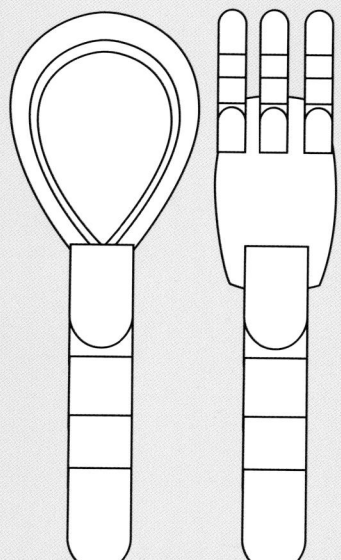

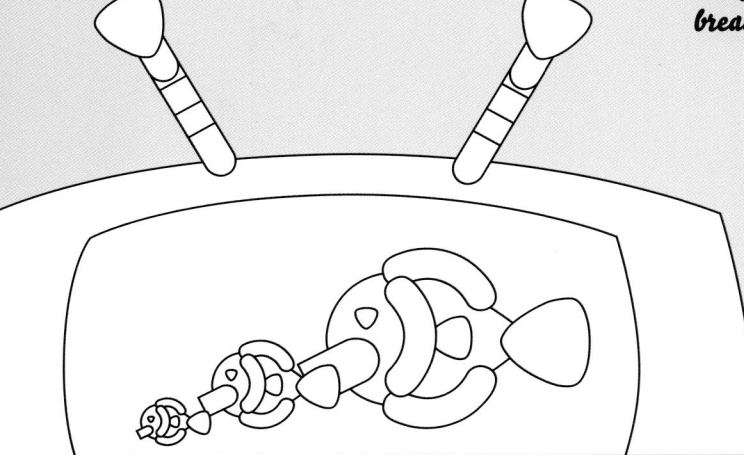

"My main challenge was trying not to break the rules, and break them at the same time!"

For this piece I used a lot of blending, grouping and overlapping. Not too many colours though, as this takes away from the overall clean feel. First, I visualized the shapes with which I would be able to create what I wanted. Then I analyzed all the possibilities between those shapes. From that point on, it became as simple as mix and match.

Of course, the outcome must be something easily understood. Therefore I did some extra research and sketching on the idea and conceptual level. And I do mean EXTRA! My main challenge was, quite simply, trying not to break the rules, and break them at the same time! Vormator reminded me of a famous quote by Ludwig Mies van der Rohe saying "Less is more".

Color Monster

designer: Ilk
location: Paris, France
website: www.ilkilkilk.com

ILK IS A *freelance artistic director in Paris, France. He grew up in the suburbs of Paris (1993) with a basketball in his hands. He is curious, in touch with everything and nothing frightens him. He expresses his ghetto rainbow colours on any surface, and works as much on photography as on graffiti or illustration. Amongst others, he has worked for impressive clients such as Nike, Lacoste, Oakley, Take2/Rockstar Games and Wad Peugeot.*

"My own mother was the inspiration for the colour palette in this illustration."

My illustration is a snake monster that eats colours in order to make beautiful things for the eyes. This monster is like my mother, how strange!

To give the piece more and beautiful colours, I used transparencies. This generates subtle new colours in the piece. I did not blend or group any of the Vormator Elements, but just placed them on top of each other, as it was forbidden to create new forms out of the Elements. No other manipulations were used to create the piece. I decided not to use all of the Elements because I found some of them ugly. My own mother was the inspiration for the colour palette in this illustration.

To create this piece I basically put in around 20 minutes of freestyle graphic design with the Vormator Elements. Freestyle is how I normally design as well, so it was not that different from my usual working method. I do not think that the Vormator project was a big challenge, but it was a really fun concept to work on.

Spring Wind

designer: Ins
location: Budapest, Hungary
website: www.insgraphizm.com

INSgraphizm is the *personal brand of Zoltan Szalay aka INS, for everything related to design. In 1993 INS started doing computer graphics on a C64, and in 1994 he became involved in graffiti. He also made music with two of his friends under the name Random Soundz. He has made over two-hundred flyers for underground parties due to his connections in the partyscene. It was during these years that he gradually left graffiti behind. INS started exploring new styles and techniques in the field of computer graphics.*

In 2002 he *started working at Carnation and in 2004 he founded his own design studio called DRED with 3 of his friends. Vivid colours, movement and strong visual effects mark his style. In his works you can find abstract 3D, vectors, programmed elements, bright colours, street styles, textures and strong typography.*

"The Drops were randomly positioned by an Adobe® Flash® program."

My Vormator piece shows colourful random Drops symbolizing leaves in the wind on a spring night somewhere in the East, opposed by sharp black forms and a complex Vormator typography. I only used three Elements: the Cobra for the shuriken and for the Vormator typo, the Drop for the flowing leaves and the Wurst for the bold symbol in the back.

I started out by trying to create new forms out of the eight basic Elements. This turned into a Vormator typography, and a number of other forms. From these shapes I only used the shuriken. After coming up with the typography I defining the colour palette. Later on came the leaves and the shuriken. I used transparencies to give the image a richer, three-dimensional look and to add some depth. The Drops were randomly positioned by an Adobe® Flash® program.

Usually I prefer to work with more forms but the rules of Vormator boosted my creativity very positively. The main challenge was to restrict myself using my everyday methods yet still creating something fascinating. In the course of commercial work, designers are limited by many restrictions. Therefore I usually like it when there are no rules. However if you are low on inspiration, a few simple rules can lend you a helping hand.

Zazzlepant

designer: Jeffrey Pidgeon
location: California, USA
website: www.jeffpidgeon.com

Jeff Pidgeon has *worked in the animation industry for twenty-one years. Starting as a character designer for Ralph Bakshi's "Mighty Mouse: The New Adventures", he has also worked on "Tiny Toon Adventures", "Tazmania" and "The Simpsons". He joined Pixar Animation Studios in 1991 to help develop "Toy Story", and has since worked in the story department on "Toy Story 2", "Monsters, Inc.", and the Oscar-nominated short films "Mike's New Car" and "Lifted". He is currently storyboarding on "Toy Story 3", has begun a designer toy line. Jeff is married to Swazzle's writer/puppeteer Anita Coulter. They live in northern California.*

"..., a bit like a cherry atop an ice cream sundae."

THE SUBJECT OF my piece is an elephant and his friend, a tiny bird. Even though birds don't usually stay with elephants this way (as they do with Rhinoceroses), I think I was drawn to do it because there was a good size and colour contrast between the two. The bird as a whole became a nice accent to the large shapes and dark colours of the elephant. I hope the viewer's eyes roam about the figures in a circle – starting with the elephant's face, up to the bird, and back around the body again, maintaining a balance of interest.

I usually work in an improvisational way – discovering the subject, adjusting and finessing the image as I go. I fiddled about with the shapes to decide what kind of image I wanted to create. I'm not sure how I came up with the elephant – maybe the sausage-like shapes suggested a trunk to me early in the process. Overall, it was a bit like working with the colourforms or LEGO® toys I had as a child – you take a set group of shapes and build something else out of them.

I love flat colours and simple shapes, so I really wasn't inhibited by the limitations. The biggest challenge was to decide which shapes I wanted to define with colour (like the elephant's ears against its body), and which ones I wanted to combine with the same colour into more complex shapes (as with much of the body itself). I decided to use contrasting colours to define the identity of a shape against another one. This colour palette, aside from guiding the viewer's eye about the piece, also helps describe the subjects and define their personalities. The bird ended up being a nice scale and colour contrast to the elephant, a bit like a cherry atop an ice cream sundae.

To create the shapes, I stacked Elements atop one another, combining several similarly-coloured shapes to create larger, more complex ones (like the majority of the elephant itself) with the new negative spaces. I also rotated several of the Elements to help suggest different forms (the beak of the bird, as opposed to the elephant's eyes). I also used size scaling in a similar manner, as well as to create a slight suggestion of perspective. I used many of the available Elements, as it allowed me to maximize the range of graphic complexity, scale and texture in the piece. I did not find transparency necessary, due to the subject matter.

I do not really think that this project influenced my working methods. This was very reminiscent of design projects that I would have in college, and I approached this in much the same way that I approach any design assignment. Using Adobe® Illustrator® made it simple to change the orientation, size and colour of the Elements, so creating this piece was a relaxing and enjoyable challenge, like doing a crossword puzzle on a weekend.

I think my main goal in the process was to create an appealing image while disguising the limitations that I had. I want the viewer to feel that I had all the Elements I needed, rather than to sense deficiencies due to the project's parameters.

Cyclops

designer: Jim Nelson
location: Chicago, Illinois, USA
website: www.theispot.com/artist/jnelson

JIM NELSON'S WORK has appeared in numerous games, books and magazines for both children and adults. He has been represented in the juried annual "Spectrum: The Best in Contemporary Fantastic Art" both as artist and art director and he has won awards for his work as a graphic designer. His artistic influences range from Rembrandt to Beksinski and from Klee to Kandinsky, with many stops in-between. Jim's lifelong affection for comics and cartoons exert a tremendous influence on his work. He loves animals, football, tikis and music but hates lima beans. One day he would like to visit the merry old land of Oz but for now, Jim lives and works in Chicago, Illinois.

"I usually begin any project by sketching and in this case, playing with various combinations of the Vormator Elements served as the initial 'sketching' period."

THE IDEA FOR this picture suggested itself during the process of creating it. It depicts a Cyclops who has discovered a rare and beautiful object, which he examines with interest. The picture developed very organically. I began by playing with simple combinations of the eight Vormator Elements, manipulating and combining them to create new forms. It quickly became apparent that the Elements weren't limiting at all and I was able to generate almost any shape I desired. In fact, it wasn't even necessary to use all eight Elements to create the image, although I used most of them.

I usually begin any project by sketching and in this case, playing with various combinations of the Vormator Elements served as the initial "sketching" period. I wanted to see what the Elements would suggest to me rather than trying to bend them to a preconceived idea from the start. The basic shapes of the Cyclops and his object emerged from that "sketching" period and I began composing the picture using them as a starting point. After establishing the basics of the piece, I created a rough sketch to use as a template for the rest of the composition.

I placed the sketch in Adobe® Illustrator® and began refining the shapes of the character and adding more elements to the design. I worked in black and white, but kept colour in mind, knowing it would be introduced later. I prefer working this way because it allows me to focus entirely on design and composition. As the picture evolved, so did the forms of the Cyclops. For example, his head began as an enlarged version of the Drop but eventually it was composed of two Drop Elements, not just one. His eye shifted position, his teeth changed shape, etc.

Once the main elements of the picture had been established, I began creating the smaller, secondary shapes and modifying existing forms. The thin, linear shapes that echo the form of the figure were created by making copies of the larger forms, shifting their positions, and then subtracting one from the other. My goal was to create a picture that would contain easily recognizable Vormator Elements as well as shapes that were created from those Elements but very different from them. By duplicating, enlarging, reducing, rotating, merging and subtracting the eight Elements, I was able to create complex curves, straight edges, etc. It was not unlike using a set of French curves and a straight edge to draw new shapes. I rotated and lined up the curved edges of several Elements to create curves that didn't exist within any single Element. The more shapes I created, the more tools I had to create, since new shapes could be used to add or subtract from older ones.

I included the Cyclops' inner anatomy as a means of breaking up some of the larger forms in the character. Creating the complex curves of his brain and inner organs proved to be the most challenging part of the project, but I felt they were worth the effort.

Once the final composition was in place, I enlarged and intersected a few of the original eight Elements to create the simple curves in the background. Then I began converting the black-and-white design into colour. Transparencies were employed to divide shapes and introduce more rhythm into the composition. I added gradients to soften forms and create subtle variations in colour. The colours themselves were chosen to unify the picture, provide mood and create areas of emphasis.

Looking for Love

designer: Joey Carrapichano
location: Hamburg, Germany
website: www.eo-art.com

JOEY CARRAPICHANO WAS born in Mozambique and grew up in Johannesburg. He attended college in Durban where he attained a degree in Fine Arts. He has worked in the film industry in the art department and completed the short film "The Spirit of Cain". Joey won a Best Director award at the N.T.V.A. awards in 1994 for his music video for Lithium's "Schizophrenia". Later that year Joey moved to Hollywood and pursued a career in animation and film as a digital artist. After ten years in the United States he met Sarah Laban and moved with her to Hamburg, focusing on his personal art while gaining reputation for his commercial work. Today Joey works both in Los Angeles and Hamburg, creating characters, illustrations and animations.

My concept is based on the theme "looking for love in all the wrong places" which I use in some of my personal work. The confused sheep has fallen in love with a bush and that makes for a funny image.

I thought for a long time about the concept of the picture. I didn't start putting shapes together until it was clear on what I was trying to achieve. Once that was figured out, I began by making some scribbles on a piece of scrap paper to get the basic idea out, then started to work in Adobe® Illustrator®. I wanted a bright colour palette. Bright colours make things happy and since the sheep is happily in love the colours fit the mood. I carefully constructed the forms out of the given Elements, sometimes using the Pathfinder tool in Adobe® Illustrator® to create new shapes. After days of tweaking, sleeping on it, tweaking more and finally adding the details, I was happy with it.

I had to decide, with the limited Elements, how to create all the shapes in my picture. First I created the background, then the characters. I wanted the point to get across easily and at first glance. It's tempting to put too much into a piece but I wanted to keep it simple. Then after all was in place, I began to add the details. Even in the simplest artwork, the devil is in the details.

My usual working method is almost the same. I come up with an idea and then I create it with whatever medium I am working with at the time. With this project there was a limited palette of Elements, which put some restrictions into the character that I designed. However, the way I went about it was much the same as any other project.

The main challenge was to get the Elements to fit my idea. Of course the picture is different from anything else I do because of them. Making the text out of all the little pieces took a lot of time too, but the restrictions actually made the whole process a lot of fun, rather like doing a puzzle. I surprised myself with things I came up with and sometimes had to destroy the whole thing and start again.

The influence of this project on my working methods was that I learned to be able to work with less. It is an exciting thing to create something new with only a few building blocks. Much like when you are a kid and you have a circle, a triangle and a square.

Go build!

"I didn't start putting shapes together until it was clear on what I was trying to achieve."

Heart of Design

designer: Juan Doe
location: Bronx, New York, USA
website: www.juandoe.com

Juan Doe is *an esoteric, high concept, lo-brow image-maker hailing from the cosmos of interpolated art and design. Disciplined in the fine arts of mental diligence and superior hand skills he exhumes the ashes of great art by deconstructing the facades of uninspiring clichés and homogenized pictures. Hell-bent on destruction, Juan Doe's art evokes flashes of memories within an anthropologic all time frame of the past, present and future all on one plate of scrumptious delight.*

I felt the Vormator project was attempting to achieve an exploration into the fundamental aspects of not only design but also any form of image-making, including the biological make up of life. In the simplest of terms: the heart of design. So I went out to build a visual anagram for it. In constructing the piece the only things I used were prosaic and blurry remembrances of aortas, right atriums, left ventricles and the physical heart in abstract terms.

In keeping with the prescribed spirit and challenge of the project I kept all my techniques to the simplest of executions, starting with choosing how many Elements I would exploit. Even though eight shapes are simple enough, I wanted to strip it down even further. I ended up using two Elements, the Cobra and the Tentacle for almost 90% of the piece. The third Element, the Badge, was used sparsely, though it is probably the most important accent because it is the only shape that constitutes the contour of our actual human heart. I found that when the Cobra and the Tentacle intertwined at a certain juncture a 3-D illusion was formed. I dubbed it "The Cobracle". I grouped this new shape and explored a couple of combinations, mostly rotating and flipping. The final execution came down to intuitive layering of the Cobracle and Tentacle and the subtle

> *"...an exercise to break away from the rigidity and complexity of overdesigning."*

composition of colour and objects. In creating the colour palette I tuned in on very warm earth tones contrasted by pink, flesh hues with orange as a loud accomplice.

I have always been a proponent of "less is more" and fundamentals are where creation begins and ends. In employing this philosophy I use a very freestyle approach to design. This project seems to follow the same sentiment, an exercise to break away from the rigidity and complexity of overdesigning. This does not imply that a complex piece cannot be created from a few elements. On the contrary, it shows how far the potential of creation can go with the simplest of forms.

The Vormator project has certainly served as a reminder that in design, especially today in the overabundant universe of image-making, there is great skill in tuning in to some fundamental basic shapes and creating up from there.

Follow Me

designer: Justin J. Austin
location: Illian, New York, USA

Justin Austin was born in New York 21 years ago and currently lives in Ohio. He is a third-year student at Youngstown State University, majoring in Graphic Design. He has been interested in art since he was about 10 years old. In high school his interest for graphic design took hold and he has loved it ever since. He does a decent amount of painting, silk-screening and is always willing to try new forms of art. He enjoys learning random bits of information and gaining inspiration from that. He feels the best way to keep being creative is to keep learning and exposing yourself to as many things as possible.

THOUGH MY WORK is fairly abstract, this piece is about visual movement and visual focal points. I tried to create a story using the Elements while still trying to retain that movement. I wanted there to be a "follow the leader" feel to it. The large red shape is leading the way with its trail in green leading back to a starting point as smaller and similar shapes follow suit. I wanted my colour palette to be mainly earth tones with powerful accents to make certain shapes of my choosing stand out more.

I played around with the Elements and decided which shapes best fit my initial idea and positioned them roughly where I wanted. After that, I started getting a little more complex. I built a few shapes out of a couple of the Elements, using the Adobe® Illustrator® Pathfinder tool. I also used the tool to cut one Zerk out of another and then grouped it with a Tentacle. After creating this grouped shape, I copied and pasted it to have multiples, then layered the two large green Cobras instead of using the Pathfinder tool. This enabled me to position the grouped Zerk shapes under one of the Cobras and over the other. Another important part of my technique is being able to change my ideas in mid-progress and evolve it into something different. I also like to group objects that have some relation to other shapes. There are three brown Zerk shapes that I have grouped so I can easily move them without having to adjust every one individually.

I developed my idea by doing rough thumbnail drawings in a sketch book to play with different variations without having to commit a lot of time to ideas that might not work out. After narrowing it down to some of my favourites I took them more seriously and started to work on the computer, positioning them and fitting things together. Deciding where things went worked best when I kept in mind where and what was going to be which colour. When the foundation was layed down, I started tweaking different positions and colours until I got the end result.

My usual working method lent itself well for this project. Having only eight shapes to work with made it difficult to decide what to do. So I began playing around with various ideas of arrangement by doing quick thumbnails like I normally do. Then I started to play around with the thumbnails I did in my sketchbook on the computer. Like most of my work, this piece started out as a small idea and as I made progress I added more to it. I am finished with a piece, when I feel that adding anything else will ruin it.

The most difficult thing about this project was having only eight shapes that you could not change very much. I had to rely mainly on the Elements themselves to achieve what I wanted rather than special effects or anything of that sort. It forced me to work with set objects: I couldn't just make up what I needed to fit the piece. I had to find solutions to this visual problem through those eight shapes. This limited creativity in one sense but forced me to be more creative with the Elements.

> *"A lot of designers get caught up being flashy and tend to overwhelm the real essence of their goal."*

The Vormator project showed me how important the basic elements of design are. A lot of designers get caught up being flashy and tend to overwhelm the real essence of their goal. There is basic ground work that needs to be understood: how shapes relate to each other and how colour, movement and size play major roles in good design. This project showed me that a designer can come up with almost anything with only a few elements. The only thing that can limit us is how far we are willing to take our ideas.

Self-Portrait

designer: Justin Kok
location: Montréal, Canada
website: www.justinkok.com

JUSTIN KOK WAS *born and lives in Montréal. He began his studies in Digital Arts at Vanier College and holds a Bachelor of Fine Arts degree in Design Art from Concordia University. His work has been previously presented in Montréal at the Société des arts technologiques and the Flow/Courant exhibit at Séquence in Chicoutimi. Justin is currently designing for a clothing company whose headquarters is in Montréal, Canada. His work is noted for tempting the viewer with a sense of playful intrigue while drawing from the simplicity of the everyday.*

THE PIECE IS a self-portrait. I chose to use this particular image because of its intriguing composition and clearly defined central focus. The technique I used most prominently in the piece was a stippling effect. Most of the other Elements were used throughout the illustration in combination, except for the Cobra. My intent was to make as subtle use of the forms as possible.

A black and white colour palette was chosen to emphasize the shading, and to not detract from the feel of the piece. Choosing a source image was my first task, so it was important to choose a photograph with detail and good contrast in mind to facilitate the production of the stippling effect.

When faced with the eight Elements that would be used for the project, the first decision I made was which of the shapes would be used to shade the composition. The Chevron was chosen because of its versatility. Using it in multiples with aligned rotation, it could be used for outlines, and because of its shape it was also ideal for directional shading to emphasize the illusion in the apple, hand, hoodie and facial areas of the illustration. It was important to concentrate on the part of the illustration that would later become the focus of the piece, so I spent extra effort rendering these areas.

To create the stippling effect, a Chevron was reduced to a miniscule size, and duplicated. Each multiple of the Chevron was individually placed, and rotated without the use of scatter brushes or patterns to create shading effects, and outlines: the denser the spacing of the Chevrons, the darker the apparent shade and the opposite for lighter shades.

"Shading the piece was meticulous."

Shading the piece was meticulous. The process mostly went as follows: Zoomed in as far as I could go, I would select a Chevron, duplicate, move and rotate it. After repeating a dozen times or so,

I would zoom out to monitor the progress, zoom back in to correct, or continue the process. The same process was used in the outlines.

Forms were combined using the Adobe® Pathfinder® tool to create the solid areas of the hair and track-jacket and these were highlighted using the same stippling effect. The details of the hoodie were rendered using only the Chevron to help contrast with the solid shapes of the tracksuit jacket.

Blends were avoided wherever possible, but were used in a few instances to achieve the naturally smooth curves found in the drawstrings of the hoodie and zipper tracks of the jacket, and the stripes found in the tracksuit jacket. For the drawstrings and zipper tracks, the Drop was used, and the Bar was used for the stripes.

My regular working method differs from the one I used for this project. I am not usually as meticulous and precise when it comes to compositions but usually allow compositions to flow from themselves, but it definitely was refreshing and inspiring to compose so purposefully.

The biggest challenge in creating this piece for the Vormator project was to use the forms as subtly as possible while keeping within the project's guidelines. The challenge in effect was to convince the viewer that there was more to the piece than initially thought.

The Vormator project has greatly influenced the way I design. It allowed for a good opportunity to work outside of my comfort zone, and I felt the project was successful in exercising both my creative and technical skills in a balanced way.

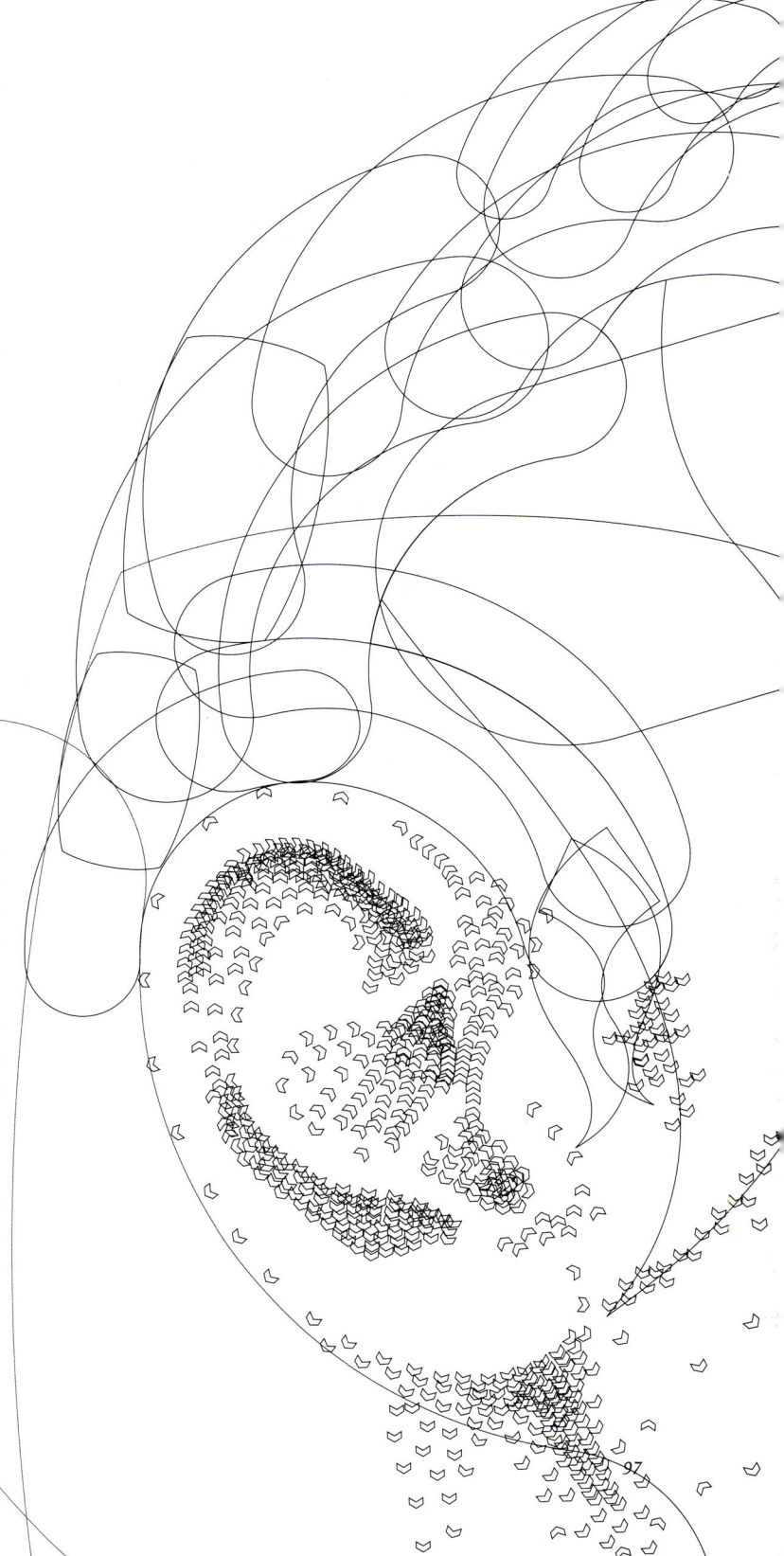

Most Likely a Donkey

designer: Keisuke Omi
location: San Francisco, California, USA
website: www.keisukeomi.com

Keisuke Omi is *a user interface designer based in San Francisco, CA. He puts emphasis on information architecture, visual design, and localization within a fast-paced, collaborative, and challenging environment that encourages innovation. He is sensitive to the needs of Japanese end-users, clients and developers. SpikeSource, an US-based company, is Keisuke's current employer. Keisuke designs and prototypes user interfaces for customer-facing web presences, back-office applications, and maintenance tools shipped with core product. He is also responsible for corporate and product branding.*

THIS PIECE MOST likely represents a donkey but there is an equal chance that it is a fat horse or a zebra. I don't think that what it is, is very important in this.

Only seven out of eight Elements were used. Lacking any curves, the Chevron felt out of place amongst the others and was not useful in creating the organic shape. The elements that were used were manipulated only by size and angle. I wanted to keep the elements recognizable, so I stayed away from performing Boolean operations to create new shapes. I tried not to shrink or enlarge the elements too much for the same reason.

Most of the Elements were filled with a flat colour with a slight transparency – no gradients or patterns – because I thought that the overlaps added enough complexity and points of interest. A popping colour was chosen to try to direct some attention to the negative space.

> "Think before you leap."

First I defined the problem. The goal of a design – in general – should be to solve a problem. I believe that there are no wrong problems but there are wrong solutions to a given problem. In this case the problem that needed to be solved was well defined by the 'customer' in a language that designers can understand, which is rare.

After having determined the problem I identified the best solution: Think before you leap. There should always be a single best solution for a given problem. I always spend time on this step so that resources are not wasted during the next steps. Chicken-scratch is the way to go.

An important step in this and every other design I make, is reviewing the design and identifying what works well. Some parts should be kept while the rest can be removed. Get feedback from colleagues and customers if possible. You need to examine the design to make sure that nothing was missed. The last step was to clean up the design, pack it, and send it off on time.

Design is problem solving and it was no different for this project. There are always constraints and restrictions. These days it is rare that I complete a project from start to finish on my own. The experience was liberating, but felt a little lonely at the same time. It was difficult to know when to stop – I could have been making tiny adjustments forever. I figured the piece was ready for submission when the number of changes that were undone started exceeding the number of changes that were committed. Design is fun, and the Vormator project was no exception.

Vormator Generative #143

designer: Kyle Phillips
location: Minneapolis, Minnesota, USA
website: www.workofkylephillips.com

"...multi-purpose vector artwork at the push of a button."

Designer Spotlight

Kyle Phillips is an artist interested in traversing the boundaries of New Media and Graphic Design. Fascinated by the pragmatic and aesthetic possibilities of new media synthesis, he explores the potential of programmatic strategies in his work as an integral facet of design process and problem solving. His work often utilizes new media to create collaborative toolsets in which users have the ability to take an active part in his work, involving them on variable levels of authorship and allowing for the open-ended evolution of continuous live projects.

Kyle Phillips is currently a student at the Minneapolis College of Art and Design where he studies Interactive Media under his advisor and mentor Piotr Szyhalski. Kyle has been a freelance commercial artist for four years and has also held exhibitions and live performances in a variety of local forums. His work includes print, web and interactive design and he is currently working in tandem with DesignWorks, MCAD's in-house studio, on the incorporation of his generative strategies into MCAD's award-winning Identity system.

Vormator Generative #143 is one of over two hundred graphics created using a generative compositional engine for the Vormator project. It is a chaotic image that embraces chance and unpredictability based on rational structure principals. The images explore composition in terms of rules and object (element) relationships developed within complex organic systems.

The Vormator Elements were used as the visual assets for the culmination of a year-long project in generative design. The shapes were integrated into the compositional engine and used for the entire development phase. Most Elements were left in their original state; their patterns and hierarchical relationships were emphasized. The generative compositional engine into which the objects were placed is a modular application that is extensive and allows for various libraries of assets. The final result is an application that creates multi-purpose vector artwork at the push of a button.

The engine incorporates three main modules; one that allows the user to choose the assets, one that manages colour and one that plots coordinates and builds the composition. User settings, compositional rules and a level of chaos determine the final outputs. The project began by researching composition, taking common principles like the golden mean and rule of thirds. I then had to interpret these into logical conditions; every composition has a focal point, a direction of movement and a hierarchy; a logical reason for its results.

My work always starts with research, followed by visual exercises. After conducting the research, I draw concept sketches and then execute these on the computer. I frequently print proofs and sketch what I would like to see on top. With this project there were many additional steps. After building the basic toolsets for the engine, I analyzed each Element and envisioned different patterns in which they could be employed. I did this for each Element, building patterns and relationships and attaching them to the different assets. After the asset patterns were developed, different methods of plotting coordinates were created to allow a greater range of underlying structures in the final outputs.

The main challenge in this project was getting all of the different Elements to come together and finding a cohesive balance between the control and chaos. It was necessary to implement enough rules to make the compositions consistently effective while still allowing the system to be open enough so that there could be significant variation.

The Vormator project and my engine have heavily influenced the ways that I design. It has revealed new methods of creation, provided a different understanding of composition and programming and has helped me explore the potential of multi-functional applications and develop a powerful tool that has an infinite lifespan, is effective for branding, print, video, and web and has allowed me to explore and contrast the principles of implementation in each.

"I aim to be surprised, and to surprise others."

Designer Spotlight

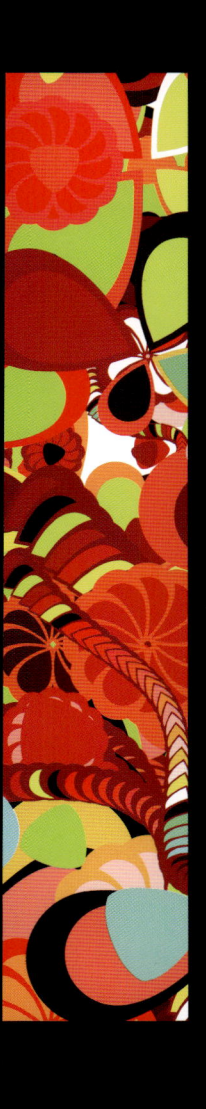

The work I create often involves a computational approach to design, I utilize programming to engage the audience in my work and allow them to collaborate with the piece. I enjoy creating projects where interaction is the focus, giving the project a life of its own and the ability to experience something different each time. The projects I like to work on are physical installations that react to the user's presence, and web collaborations where the user is able to create something new.

Adobe® Flash® was chosen as the ideal environment for the development of the engine because of its strength in handling vector objects and the ease of developing each module in separate files, allowing for future functionality and asset libraries to be easily created. Developing in Adobe® Flash® also has made it possible for the engine to be showcased online allowing anyone to generate his own graphics with the "Generative Engine." I work with a lot of different technologies and especially enjoy developing with Adobe® Flash® and Processing.

To start the creation of my Generative Engine I had to determine the functionalities that would be required in order to make a flexible toolset and develop utilities for the user's control. The Generative Engine is comprised of three main modules for user control, one that provides control over the composition's colours, one that provides control over the assets to be used, and the relational scale of each asset and one that provides different methods of plotting coordinates and control over density of the composition. Once the button is pressed to generate a new composition, artwork begins to plot itself using the selected preferences. Each object that is placed onto a coordinate then iterates a selected pattern; for instance the Drop Element selects whether it wants to be a "flower", a "propeller", or a "sine wave." Each object also follows compositional rules to establish relationships with the other objects and the scale of each object is based on its distance from the compositions focal point.

With my work I aim to be surprised, and to surprise others, I like to create unexpected experiences and arrive at unique solutions to a communication problem. With this project it was the chaos that made it a success, it will never create the same composition twice and I always remain excited to see the outcome.

My interest in programming and design started as a teenager where I began familiarizing myself with design and its tools as well as developing websites and beginning to learn Adobe® Flash® and some basic C++. I tended to go back and forth between programming and designing and was unaware of their mutual ground. Since then I have focused on Interactive Media and its unification with design, have studied at the Minneapolis College of Art and Design and have been given the opportunities to work on projects for clients like Coca-Cola and Adobe® Systems.

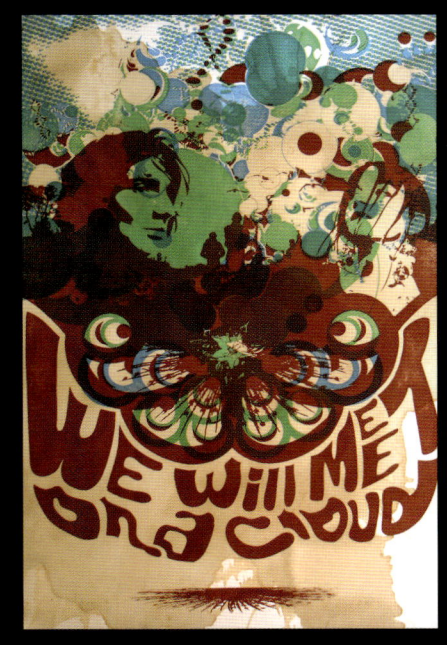

Baum-Arbol-Tree

designer: Lala Ladcani
location: Buenos Aires, Argentina
website: www.flickr.com/photos/tedementa

LALA WAS BORN in 1983 and always lived on the outskirts of Buenos Aires, surrounded by train tracks. A formal early education in a German school combined with art, design and advertising studies were the starting point for the search for a personal visual style; A universe made up of photographs from other times, an ironic revision of childhood and a particular fetish for strange objects from other places added to a genuine interest in electronic music and cutting edge design.

FOR SEVERAL YEARS she worked for different design studios and advertising agencies and currently designs a magazine on technology and trends in Argentina. At present she contributes illustrations for several books and magazines under the name "Te de Menta" (Mint Tea) and creates objects that complement her ideal world, such as tote bags, pillow covers with serigraphy and custom gloves.

I tried to create just a shape union because I feel that this made the piece more fun. First I analyzed each Element in detail and started to make tests; some of those tests were "more friendly" to me than others because of the rounded ends or because their simplicity allowed me to create things that do not necessary reveal their origins. I chose primary colours and basic shapes. Usually, my personal work is also based on those primary colours; that way I felt comfortable using them. Many Elements have the potential to become millions of different things. I performed many tests, mostly just for fun, until I finally decided to create a wood with

> *"Many Elements have the potential to become millions of different things."*

characters. My intention was to work only with shapes and colours. I tried not to use transparencies or blends, which proved to be quite a challenge.

My usual working method is similar to working with the Elements even though I have many non-vector handmade works. I believe Vormator is a good way of discovering new shapes. The slogan sounded interesting to me because one clear and strict slogan helps focus imagination in the piece.

Pill Explosion Causes Happiness

designer: Lindedesign (Christian Lindemann)
location: Hannover, Germany
website: www.lindedesign.de

Christian Lindemann was born in 1975 and grew up in a small town in Germany. He was inspired to take up graphic design and illustration as a result of his lifelong passion for drawing. He began to develop his skills at an early age and formed his own style while studying at universities in Germany and Australia. Afterwards he had 3 years' working experience as a full time graphic designer at an advertising agency.

Since October 2007 he has been working as a freelance Illustrator and graphic designer for clients including eBay, DHL, Yello Strom, Mitsubishi and TNT. As a result his work has been exhibited in Europe and abroad, appeared in numerous magazines like Computer Arts, books such as Tres Logos and Pictoplasma and has been featured on many websites.

My illustration does not have a specific theme or meaning. I was just trying to have some fun with the Elements. And, like most of my work, it is a colourful character design. Pill explosion causes happiness!

I decided to work strictly within the guidelines of the Vormator project (no new Elements, no transparencies, and so on) because that limitation represented the main challenge and fun of the project. So I tried to create my piece with all the given Elements. There was one Element, the Chevron, that went unused – just because it was not needed in the design. To make it also a bit more graphical I used only four colours with bright, attractive contrasts. None of the Elements needed manipulation.

> *"Suddenly a character appeared and after a while the shapes started to take form."*

The biggest and important step for me was to start, and to get into it. Because of the limitations, it was a bit tricky to find the best way to create the illustration. At first I drew out some rough sketches but they were not very helpful. I took a break and started just playing around with some of the Elements in Adobe® Illustrator®. Suddenly a character appeared and after a while the shapes started to take form.

Normally I make a sketch of what I have in mind or just out of the blue. When I´m happy with what I have done, I begin to rebuild the drawing in Adobe® Illustrator® until I think the piece is finished. This time – with the limitation of only a few specific objects – I started with a blank Illustrator® page and added all the basic Elements. I combined them and played around. Step by step the final piece took shape.

The main challenge, of course, was the low number of given Elements. Also, the limitations in the rules with respect to changing the shapes and special effects were a bit hard to deal with. As a difference with how I normally work, this was more a way of creating the artwork by trial and error than working with sketches and a specific idea.

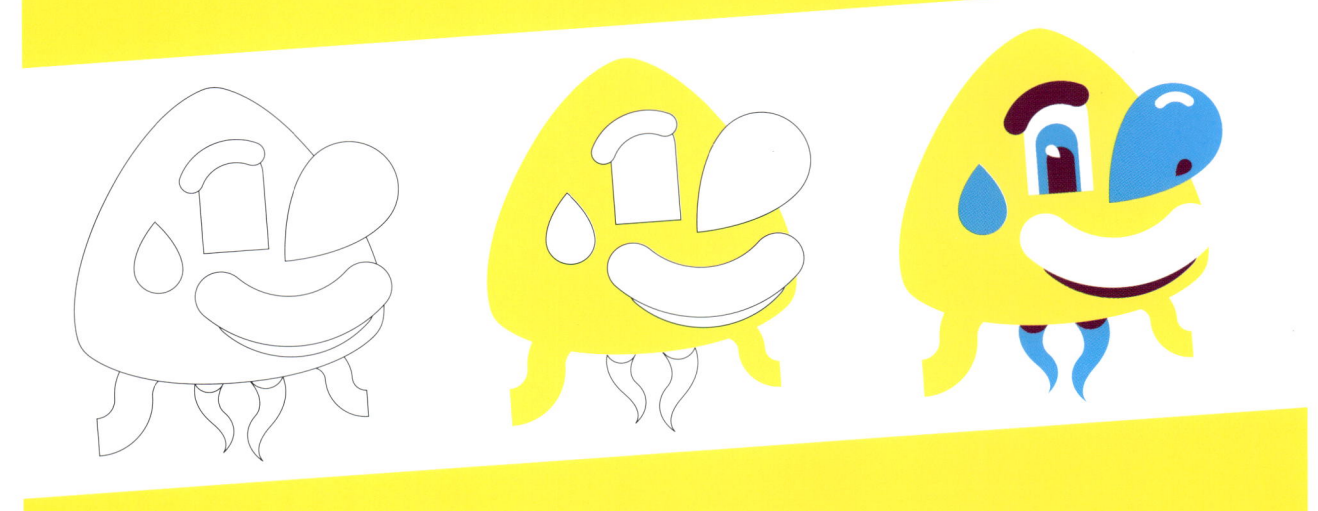

Carrot Bombs

designer: MAKI
location: Groningen, The Netherlands
website: www.makimaki.nl

MAKI IS A *design and illustration studio based in Groningen in the Netherlands. It was founded early 2005 by Kim and Matthijs, who met at the Art Academy. Their work can be described as wacky, edgy, humorous, urban and intelligent and can be found on just about anything, from clothing to walls, from plain paper to human bodies. MAKI has worked for a variety of clients all over the world, including Rockpile magazine, Laurence King publishing, 3FM radio, Computer Arts Projects and many many more.*

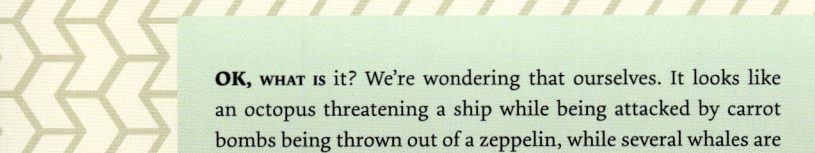

OK, what is it? We're wondering that ourselves. It looks like an octopus threatening a ship while being attacked by carrot bombs being thrown out of a zeppelin, while several whales are sleeping in the background...

We started creating several patterns by repeating the same Element in different ways. We used the patterns to create the background; water, rain and teeth. We used the Elements as they are to create new objects and characters by placing them next to each other or on top of each other. We kept things simple and brought them together with the colour scheme.

> *"Where do you start and where on earth does it end?"*

Since this technique was new to us, we started working on it like we always do; without a real plan, improvising. When we created the patterns, one of them looked like water, so this inspired the sea theme. We created different characters and shapes on the side playing with the elements and picked the ones we liked best.

Usually we draw everything by hand first and use those hand drawn images in the final product. Not using our hands was the biggest challenge. Where do you start and where on earth does it end? Now we had to use the Elements to create something in the computer. Funny though - you can still taste a MAKI flavour in it.

We soon came to the conclusion that we prefer our usual working method. We need the freedom to create whatever comes up in our minds. But it was an interesting experiment and we understand people who do work like this better now.

Le Petit Chaperon Rouge

designer: Maloo
location: London, UK
website: www.unit9.com

MALOO IS A *French graphic designer and illustrator who graduated from the ENSAAMA in Paris. She moved to England to give life to the chubby characters and surreal world living inside her head. She also wanted to experiment with living on an island and eating beans. Results are still being investigated. While studying at the Surrey Institute of Art and Design in Farnham, she spent most of her time drinking wine, missing cheese, dreaming about the big city, and freelancing for Airside from time to time. Since last summer, she has been working as a full-time designer at Unit9 in London while maintaining her freedom working as a freelance illustrator.*

This piece is a modern version of Little Red Riding hood. When I first received the Vormator brief and saw the Elements, I immediately thought of my childhood. The Elements are a mix of soft and hard,

"When I turned the Badge shape upside down I saw this little girl's cape and hat."

simple and complex shapes that together create a language that I could understand. I suddenly thought of the games I played as a child and how my imagination could construct endless buildings out of simple cubes. I started playing around with some of the shapes – turning them over, mixing them and creating new forms. When I turned the Badge shape upside down, I saw this little girl's cape and hat in a very simple and expressive way. At this point, I found my theme and started to think about the whole scene.

From the very start, this project was in harmony with my personal approach to illustration. For a few years now, the aim of my work has been to find the simplest, most dynamic and expressive way to illustrate a situation. After experimenting for a day, I discovered that the possibilities offered by these shapes were as unbound as imagination itself – with a bit of work, you could recreate any existing vector shape. But instead of going down that road, I decided to treat the Elements as independent and almost complete shapes that I could rearrange in a given space.

I decided that I would follow the spirit of simplicity in the whole artwork and try to make as few alterations as possible, using mainly transparency, colours, scaling and duplication. Finally I played around and followed my instinct to recreate the wolf and express the forest atmosphere. Once my elements were in place, I decided to set the scene during the spring, using only vibrant colours to keep the children's spirit inherent to my piece. I wanted my piece to be very soft and dreamy and to reflect the tale in its most innocent and childish way.

The main challenge for me was to try to keep the Elements as close to the originals as possible and to give them a life and my personal touch.

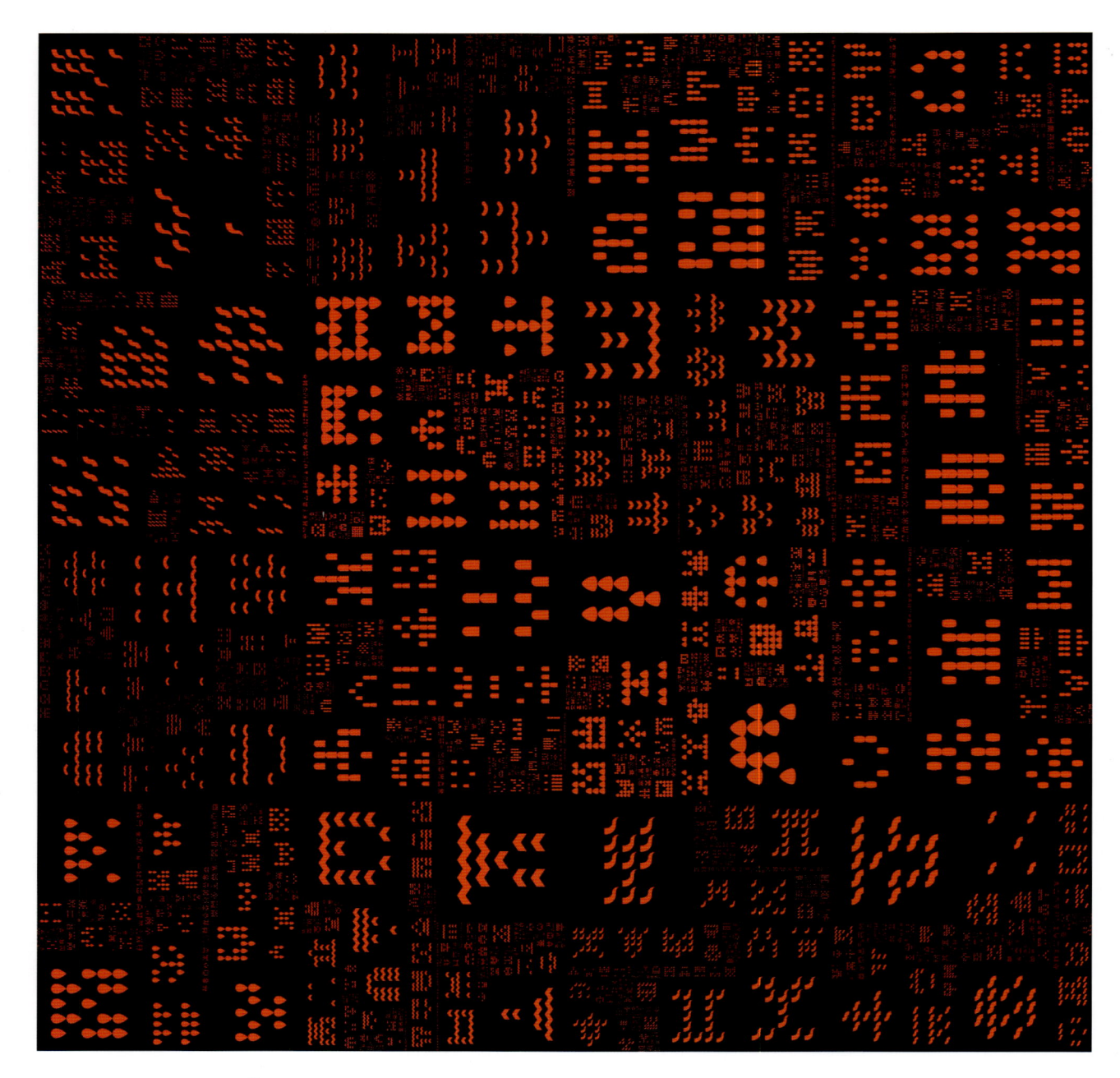

Fabric of Life

designer: Mara Ang Chong Lai
location: Singapore, Singapore
website: www.chonglai.com

Mara Ang Chong Lai is an Art Director, Illustrator and Designer by profession based in Singapore. His artwork has received numerous awards. Recently, he received a qualifier award for the Shanghai Poster Design Competition held in China. He has worked on accounts ranging from Subaru, Ford, Peugeot, Nokia, HP, Amex to Burger King. At heart, he considers himself a multi-disciplinary artist who creates artwork using experimental techniques and different ideas fused by the love to make things happen.

His work and styles are influenced by his education in Philosophy and Sociology while studying at the National University of Singapore. The artwork created for Vormator using the Elements provided is intended to reflect the philosophy of language by Ludwig Wittgenstein. The artwork hopes to explore the shapes behind typography to represent the meanings and enunciations of languages from different cultures.

The subject of the piece is language. In this piece, I have expressed the simulation of cultures. During its process, I created a form that expresses a language that transcends differences through art. Thus, this may well be how an alien language might originate within a culture. The artwork explores the beauty of words in the form of characters nested within a language.

After rearranging the Elements, they were painstakingly merged to create different forms. Each different form was then grouped into a 4 cm. x 4 cm. block. The Elements take form in blocks of two spreads across sixteen blocks. I used all the Elements because they fitted into my equation of even numbers within the layout. The red on black colour represents the bloodline of language in an unknown culture. Like a red thread woven through a black cloth, a tongue-in-cheek homage to Ludwig Wittgenstein.

Usually, I experiment with different techniques to create an artwork. As a multi-disciplinary artist, I often try to churn out as many styles as possible. Sometimes I learn from others by studying, copying and modifying other people's techniques. Most of the time I try to create more original artwork by mixing and matching traditional fine art with modern design software.

"This may well be how an alien language might originate within a culture."

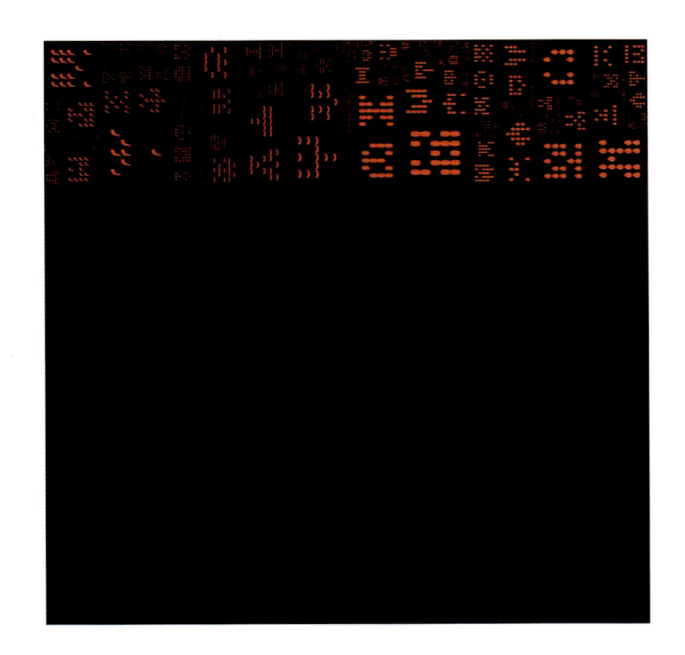

It is often the brainstorming and sketching stages that are most important to me. I mentally rearrange the different shapes and then come up with certain configurations. After that, I try to recreate an exact copy of a mental configuration with my own eyes and hands.

The main challenge for me was to create an artwork given the limited set of Elements. It almost was like letting Ockham's Razor cut an advertising brief. As the saying goes, "it is easier to complicate than to simplify". However, you can still be creative within a given framework. Simple little things can be beautiful too.

Untitled

designer: Marina Chaccur
location: São Paulo, Brazil
website: www.marinachaccur.com.br

Marina is a *Brazilian designer, who graduated from Fundação Armando Alvares Penteado – FAAP – SP (BA Design), then did a postgraduate degree at the London College of Communication (MA Graphic Design). As a freelance professional she organizes design conferences, lectures, workshops and exhibitions in Brazil and abroad.*

Ornaments and patterns have been subject of my study for a while. So when I was faced with the Vormator challenge, it was natural for me to create a sort of ornament, organized through repeated forms.

From the set of Elements I chose only the appropriate forms. To check which one suited me best I tried different arrangements. In the end only four out of the eight Elements were used; the round and curvy ones. A few of them were overlapped to create a new form, but were still recognizable as the initial Element.

These groups of Elements were placed around the centre of the document. In this way I was able to take advantage of the square document and to create a circular and symmetric layout. The process was simple in terms of actions in the software and orientated towards a visual research of combinations and repetitions of the Elements.

The Elements were selected, duplicated, reflected and angled. When something seemed interesting enough it was placed in a separate document from which the final layout was created.

When the image was complete, I considered different colour schemes. The colour palette that seemed pleasing and original was elected to be the final one.

In terms of working methods, this project pretty much reflected what I usually do in my other assignments. However, I jumped directly from the briefing to the visual research. I did not

"I jumped directly from the briefing to the visual research."

perform the research I normally do, considering it was already something that I have been studying for some time and not specifically for this project.

Working with the Elements and possible arrangements was sort of a game; a challenge to get the most out of simple forms. It was a very enjoyable experience that I would like to repeat. I also consider it to be a great design exercise and quite possibly a way to relax.

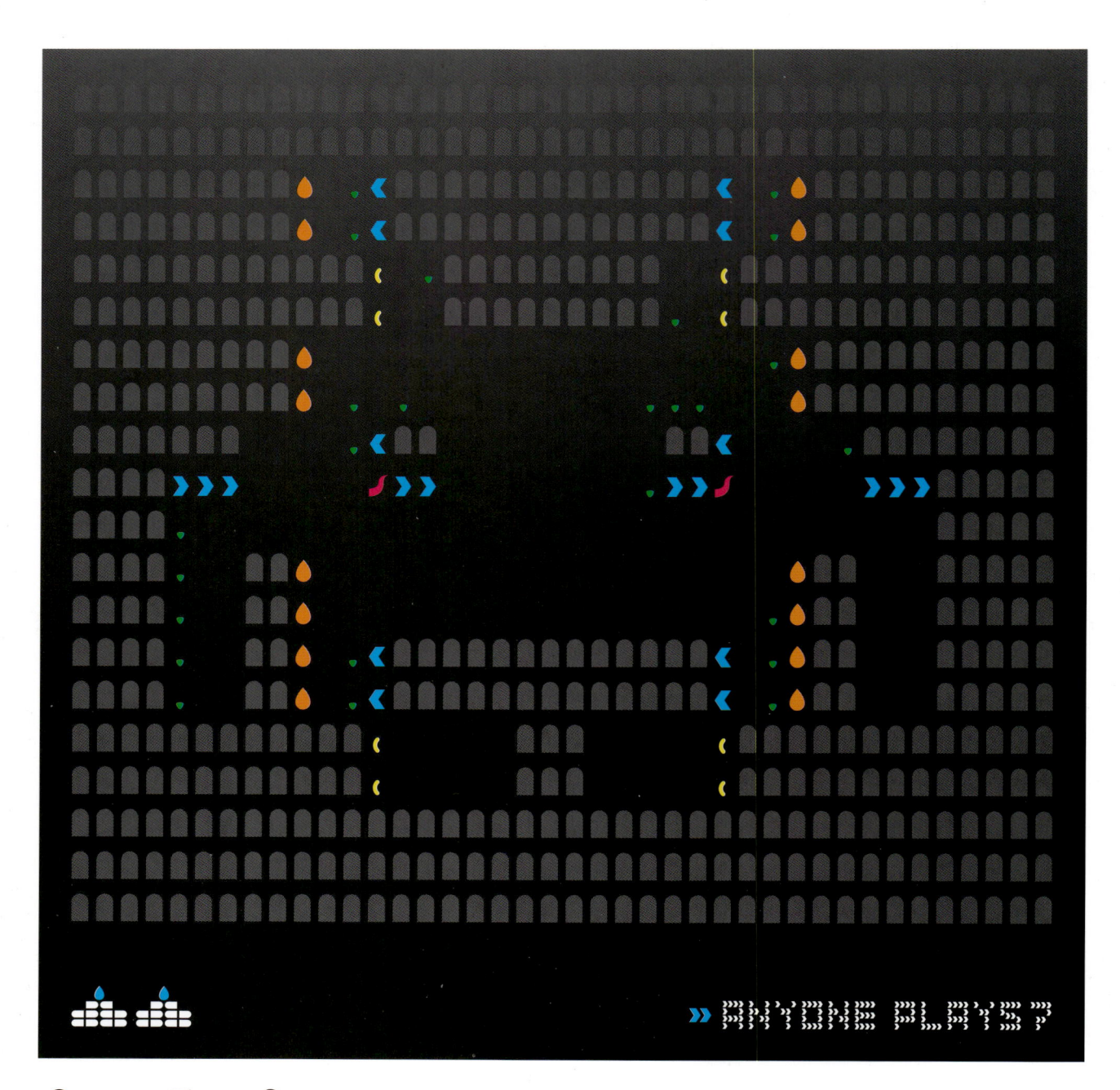

Space Invaders

designer: **Mauro Caramella**
location: **Milano, Italy**
website: www.designaside.com

CURRENTLY LIVING IN *Milan, Italy, where he completed his studies in Arts and Design, 30 year old Mauro Caramella, is now working as an art director for a leading Italian digital marketing company. He is the creator and editor of www.designaside.com, which is becoming an important site for Italian digital and non-digital art, graphics, design and photography. The site is supported by a strong community. His interests and passions include painting and photography. These have allowed him to take part in a number of exhibitions, events and publications including ContainerArt and LayerMatch.*

My artwork represents the well-known icon of the famous Space Invaders Arcade, decomposed and re-assembled to catch and to transfer the feeling of a virtual match of the game. The Arcade experience is developed using a single figure in the game. This figure was created by slicing, moving and duplicating parts of Elements and sections.

The geometric and repetitive arrangement of the Vormator Elements helped me to represent the figure. I decided to use empty spaces inside the frame instead of drawing the character directly.

First, I looked up the icon on the internet and converted this from a bitmap into an ASCII code image. Concentrating on the sequence of the characters' reproduction, I assigned shapes in the way they would better fit in the idea of the composition. Then the font was generated, replacing glyph with Vormator Elements. Finally, the new font was associated on a one to one basis with Elements to ASCII code.

The working method applied to conceive this piece is not very different from the way I usually work. Normally I start by getting the brief, trying to catch the inspiration and eventually give birth to an idea which turns into my way to express a final artwork: an image.

> *"The Arcade experience is developed using a single figure in the game."*

The hardest part of the process of creation was to replace the ASCII glyph with the graphic Elements. In order to achieve this, I needed to reduce the number of characters to a minimum without compromising the final output.

Working on a graphic project with just basic elements and shapes, although it's not always easy, has the high value of concentrating the attention of the creative job to outline the idea to an extreme synthesis. Most of the time a basic outset can produce outstanding results.

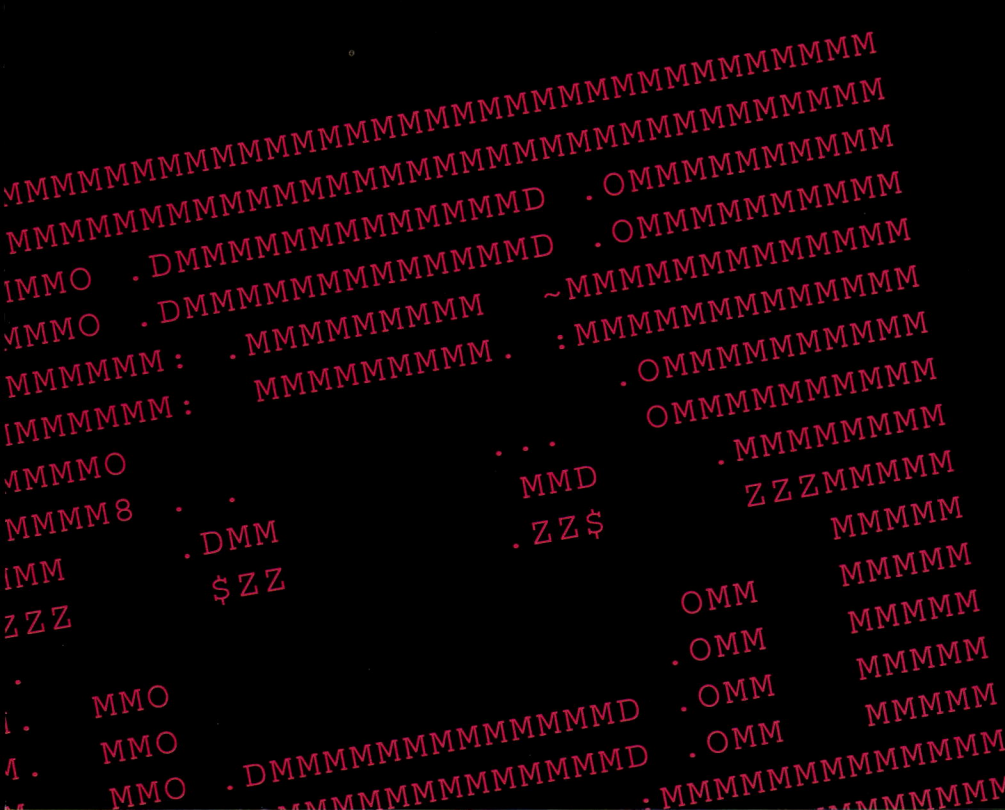

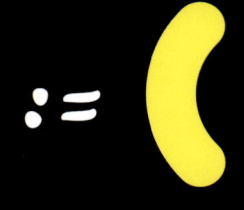

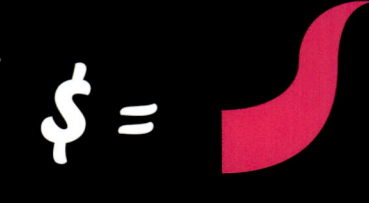

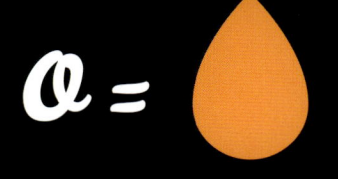

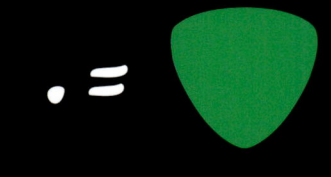

The Wurstbear Family

Designer: Meni Tzima
Location: Athens, Greece

Designer Spotlight

Meni Tzima is an illustrator living and working in Yupyland, which is a part of the Dinnerr network, located somewhere in Athens, Greece. She was born in Larisa, the hottest place in Greece in the summer, and studied design at the Technological Educational Institute of Athens. After graduating, she worked as a designer for a few months. She rapidly became attracted to illustration, which according to herself has always been her true love. She found a job as a full time illustrator working on animations for a children's educational website.

TWO YEARS LATER, she founded Dinnerr design studio together with her partner. Together, they now work on their own projects involving print, web design, animation, illustration and many more to come. She likes to work on new and exciting projects and applies her art to a range of media. Meni is regularly featured in magazines and books and has taken part in a number of exhibitions.

THIS IS THE Wurstbear family having a picnic.

Sketching and painting are in general my favorite things to do. However, character design is what I love doing the most. A walk out in the city, a random conversation, a movie, music, a good piece of art, a bad one and my everyday life are a few of the things that inspire me. All of this material breaks and melts when I sleep and the essence pours out as a good or a bad idea for new artwork. My trip to the Pictoplasma conference in Berlin provided the most inspiration for my piece.

I used mainly two Elements (the Wurst and the Zerk) because I enjoy working with curves; it represents my style. Colourwise this project was one of the weirdest things I've ever done. However, the colour palette adds to the final result.

The characters were created in relation to the Elements that I chose to work with. The next step was for my characters to interact with each other. At the same time I started working with colours and shapes, adding the final touch with my favourite part of the project: details.

The process of creation of my Vormator piece doesn't differ much from my normal working method. I enjoy working on an image as a whole and I like to place emphasis on the final details. In this sense, working on the Vormator project wasn't something unusual for my approach to the subject matter.

It was a fun and exciting project!

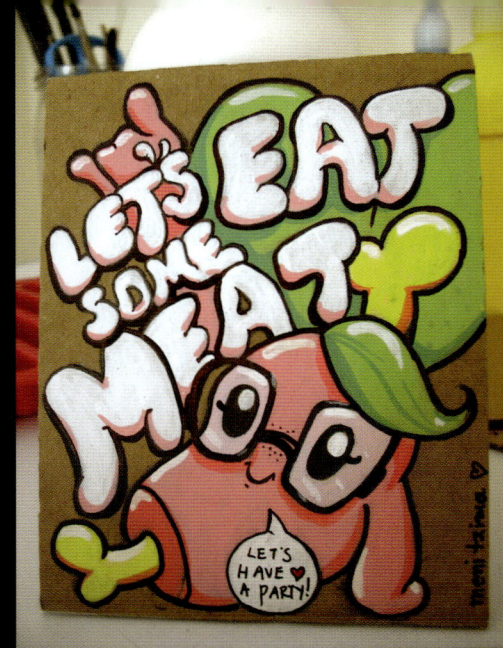

When I start working on an image, the tools I use first, are pencil and paper. I try to keep my sketchbook close to me, because I like making quick sketches of ideas that I have during the day. This could be while talking on the phone, thinking, taking decisions, and so on. This is how I usually create my roughs. I then work on these roughs some more, and make them into cleaner sketches. These are scanned and I then continue working on them and finish the job on my pc. The software I use is Adobe® Illustrator® and Photoshop® in some cases.

My plan is to keep growing Yupyland, adding more cute, silly and scary denizens to that strange place! Each character I have created, represents parts of my personality, but I think other people relate too and recognize themselves in some of those characters as well. What is important to me, is to make the viewer happy with my images. It's that simple!

Urgery

designer: Mike Pelletier
location: Banff, Alberta, Canada
website: www.pelletron.org

Mike Pelletier holds *a Bachelor of Fine Arts degree from the Alberta College of Art and Design's Media Arts and Digital Technologies Programme. He has spent the last five years working in The Banff Centre's Creative Electronic Environment, initially as the Creative Computing Technician and most recently as the manager of the Interactive Media Department. During his time at the Centre he has worked with hundreds of artists to help them realize their projects and overcome numerous complex technological hurdles. A practicing artist himself, Mike's work involves everything from drawing to videogame modifications and has been featured in exhibitions internationally.*

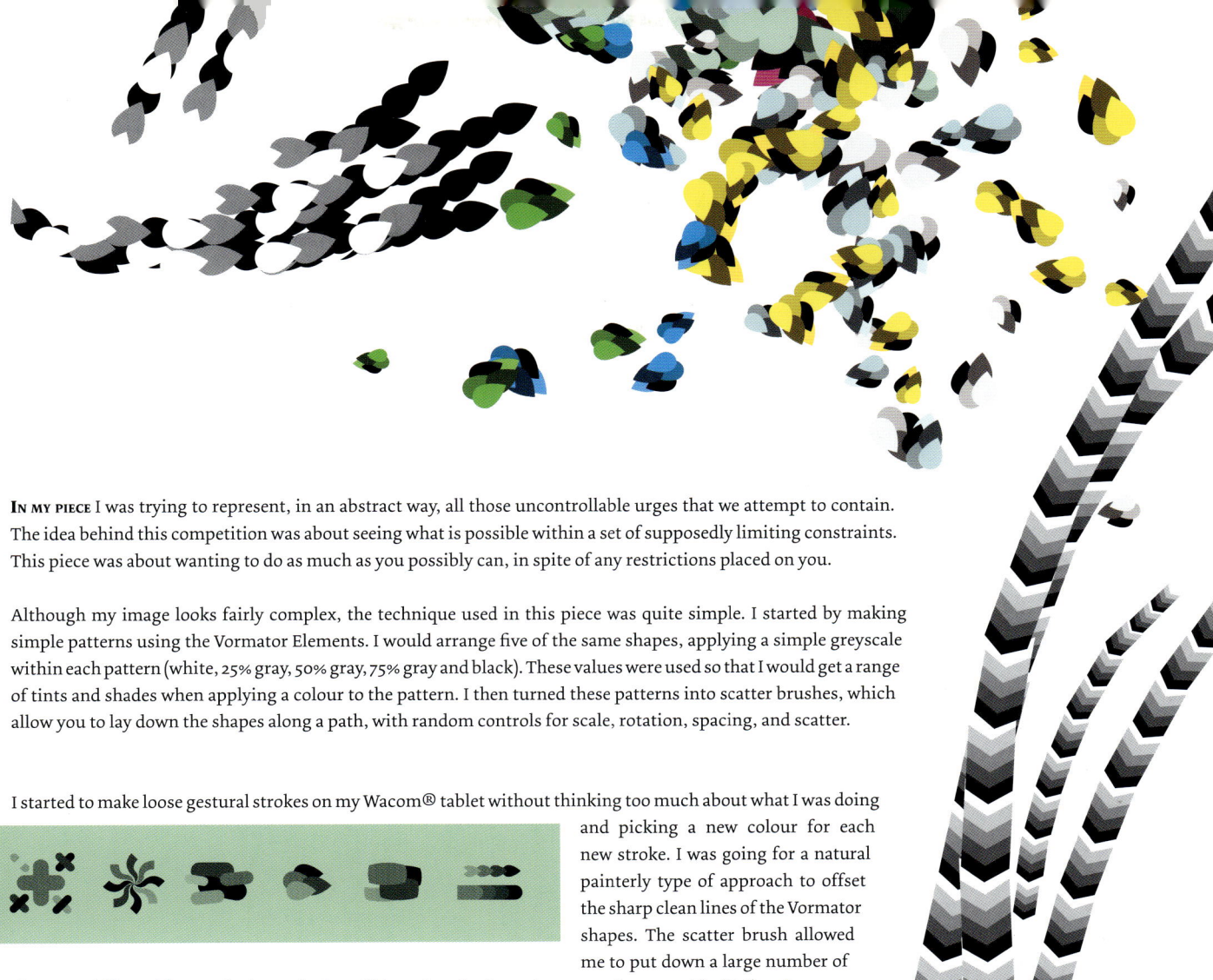

In my piece I was trying to represent, in an abstract way, all those uncontrollable urges that we attempt to contain. The idea behind this competition was about seeing what is possible within a set of supposedly limiting constraints. This piece was about wanting to do as much as you possibly can, in spite of any restrictions placed on you.

Although my image looks fairly complex, the technique used in this piece was quite simple. I started by making simple patterns using the Vormator Elements. I would arrange five of the same shapes, applying a simple greyscale within each pattern (white, 25% gray, 50% gray, 75% gray and black). These values were used so that I would get a range of tints and shades when applying a colour to the pattern. I then turned these patterns into scatter brushes, which allow you to lay down the shapes along a path, with random controls for scale, rotation, spacing, and scatter.

I started to make loose gestural strokes on my Wacom® tablet without thinking too much about what I was doing and picking a new colour for each new stroke. I was going for a natural painterly type of approach to offset the sharp clean lines of the Vormator shapes. The scatter brush allowed me to put down a large number of shapes quickly. With one single stroke I could have hundreds or shapes on the page. I built the piece up intuitively, building upon each previous stroke.

> *"The scatter brush allowed me to put down a large number of shapes quickly."*

The working method for this piece was pretty similar to what I normally do when creating artworks. I often set rules for myself, or try to work within a limited set of parameters. I start with a simple technique and create variations on that technique until something interesting happens. I also like to work with random image generators, where I make programmes that create random compositions based on a series of rules. I tried to make these sorts of techniques fit into the idea of this competition.

The biggest challenge was stopping myself! Once I got started it was pretty easy to get carried away. Before I knew it I had thousands of shapes on the page. Right from the start of the project I was really excited about the results that I was achieving. I had to exercise some restraint to make sure I wasn't going to make something insanely complex and end up with a file that would crash my machine.

This project was a good reminder that even within set of restrictions you still have the opportunity to go nuts! The rules of the project helped me get focused and cut out everything that isn't necessary. With the most simple elements and rules you can still create something complex.

Untitled

designer: Milk And Cookies
location: Brussels, Belgium
website: www.milkandcookies.be

Milk and Cookies is a small but tough interactive agency specialized in the graphic and creative side of 'the business'. They tend to do things differently. Not to be dissimilar – that's plain stupid – but to do the things they like to do in the way they like to do it and the way it deserves to be done. They know what they are best at, as a person or as a group of people, and they know how to apply that advantage for the better.

The people at Milk and Cookies enjoy the creative process that precedes the final result and, while doing so, they try not to design for design's sake, but try to think about 'the package'; how it will look and how that look will make the visitor feel – the right amount of glitter, the right kind of wrapping paper. They have four basic values while designing: Design is not a showoff. Design has to be just right. Design has to translate a feeling. Design has to get something across.

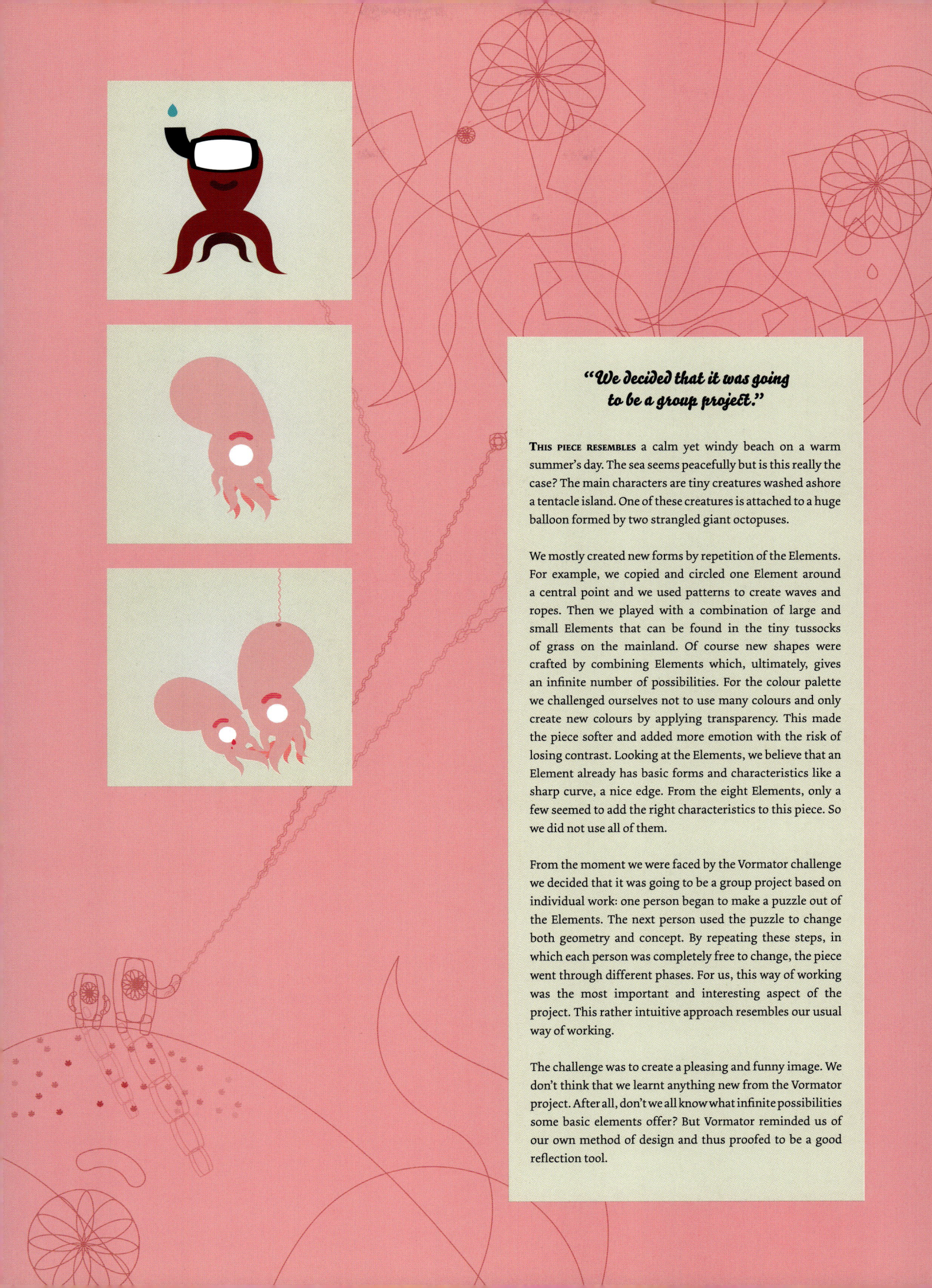

> *"We decided that it was going to be a group project."*

This piece resembles a calm yet windy beach on a warm summer's day. The sea seems peacefully but is this really the case? The main characters are tiny creatures washed ashore a tentacle island. One of these creatures is attached to a huge balloon formed by two strangled giant octopuses.

We mostly created new forms by repetition of the Elements. For example, we copied and circled one Element around a central point and we used patterns to create waves and ropes. Then we played with a combination of large and small Elements that can be found in the tiny tussocks of grass on the mainland. Of course new shapes were crafted by combining Elements which, ultimately, gives an infinite number of possibilities. For the colour palette we challenged ourselves not to use many colours and only create new colours by applying transparency. This made the piece softer and added more emotion with the risk of losing contrast. Looking at the Elements, we believe that an Element already has basic forms and characteristics like a sharp curve, a nice edge. From the eight Elements, only a few seemed to add the right characteristics to this piece. So we did not use all of them.

From the moment we were faced by the Vormator challenge we decided that it was going to be a group project based on individual work: one person began to make a puzzle out of the Elements. The next person used the puzzle to change both geometry and concept. By repeating these steps, in which each person was completely free to change, the piece went through different phases. For us, this way of working was the most important and interesting aspect of the project. This rather intuitive approach resembles our usual way of working.

The challenge was to create a pleasing and funny image. We don't think that we learnt anything new from the Vormator project. After all, don't we all know what infinite possibilities some basic elements offer? But Vormator reminded us of our own method of design and thus proofed to be a good reflection tool.

Lost Path

designer: **Mishfit**
location: **Brighton, UK**
website: **www.mishfit.com**

Michelle Maudsley, also known as Mishfit, is a flexible and dynamic designer who adapts to the diverse tasks that her roles demand. Her unique ability to bend context and distort truths have been evolving since she was old enough to hold a pencil. When the sketchbook could no longer contain the lines, they crawled their way to a page without edges… the outside world. Now Mishfit's imaginary friends exist in many forms and mediums, creating mischief wherever they go. On top of this, she enjoys travelling and getting a taste of culture, and likes to go snowboarding and mountain boarding.

With this design I wanted to create a glimpse into another world. Something more than an icon or a flat design. This is a story that you can interpret any way you like. It has four main components; the tree, the travelling girl, the blossom and the landscape. The wind plays a big part in this piece and affects all the other elements, but I like the fact that you can't see it.

I used a very straightforward process of overlapping the Elements and grouped them to create the overall shape or texture I wanted. Next I simply repeated that group of shapes as many times as was needed, using all of the original Vormator Elements except the Chevron, as its straight edges and angles would have changed the feeling of the piece. I used different alpha transparency on the leaves and bark of the tree, just to give it more texture and make it feel more convincing.

> "I was definitely inspired by a recent trip to New Zealand."

As with most of my work, it just sort of happens. I was immediately drawn to the Tentacle when I first saw the Elements. Creating a branch-like structure was a really fun thing to play around with.

Once I had the tree down, I thought it deserved a magical landscape to live in. I was definitely inspired by a recent trip to New Zealand, and wanted to recreate some of the feeling of the almost mythical landscape over there. So creating an atmosphere was really important, hence the misty cloud and subdued colours of the landscape.

Originally all of the blossom was in the tree. Because I thought that looked a little tree I added some wind, to blow the blossom around. I like the fact that you're not sure whether the blossom is being blown away from the tree or travelling on the wind towards the tree. I thought the wind would seem more real if there was someone struggling against it, so I created the girl. I think my work has a lot more impact if there is some movement in it. The whole thing just pieced together like a story really.

This process was pretty different to my normal working method as I usually start off with a sketch, especially with characters. But with the Elements, things just seemed to evolve. It was really interesting, not knowing what was going to appear next. I had to be a lot more precise than normal too; usually my work is organised chaos and quite free. However with this had to be really slick before it looked good. The slightest shape out of place was painfully obvious.

The main challenge was to get exactly the result I wanted from the restricted set of Elements and having to think laterally and sometimes use negative space to create the parts that I needed. The positioning and shape of the green hills and the path was pretty tricky, as was giving the girl clothes that didn't look awful! (I'm still not sure about her belt! I don't think I'd wear it).

It has been a really useful project, that has shown me how using a limited number of shapes can give something a really clean, tight style. I will definitely implement this technique in my future graphical work.

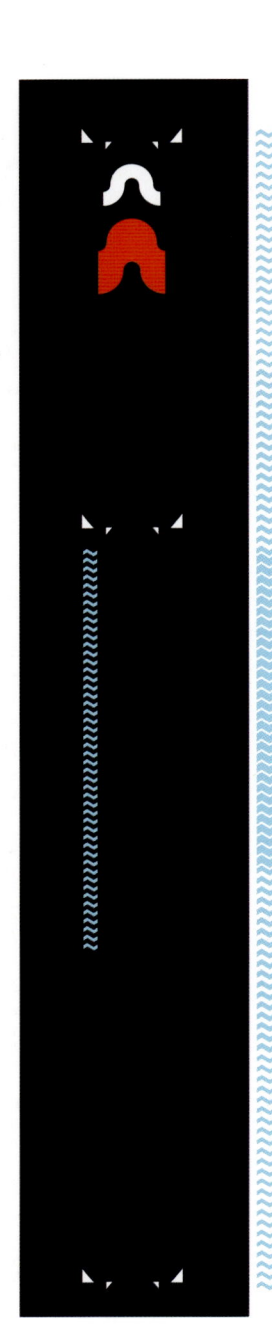

From Tokyo to Paris

designer: Mostardesign
location: Cubiac, France
website: www.mostardesign.com

MOSTARDESIGN IS AN *independent creative studio based in France, specialized in the interactive and static visual arts. The company founder, Olivier Gourvat, originally worked as a graphic designer for various agencies, producing artwork, logotypes, corporate publicities and print layouts. He later joined the team at Chronicle Editions to create image content, cover designs, illustrations and maps for numerous books on the history of the twentieth century. Following his printing experience, he pursued web design and interactive web functions, founding a website company with three associates in 1999. He established his own creative studio in 2004. The Mostardesign studio now offers innovative artistic direction, graphic design and typeface creation for clients worldwide, and has been featured in numerous publications. Olivier lives in Cubjac, France.*

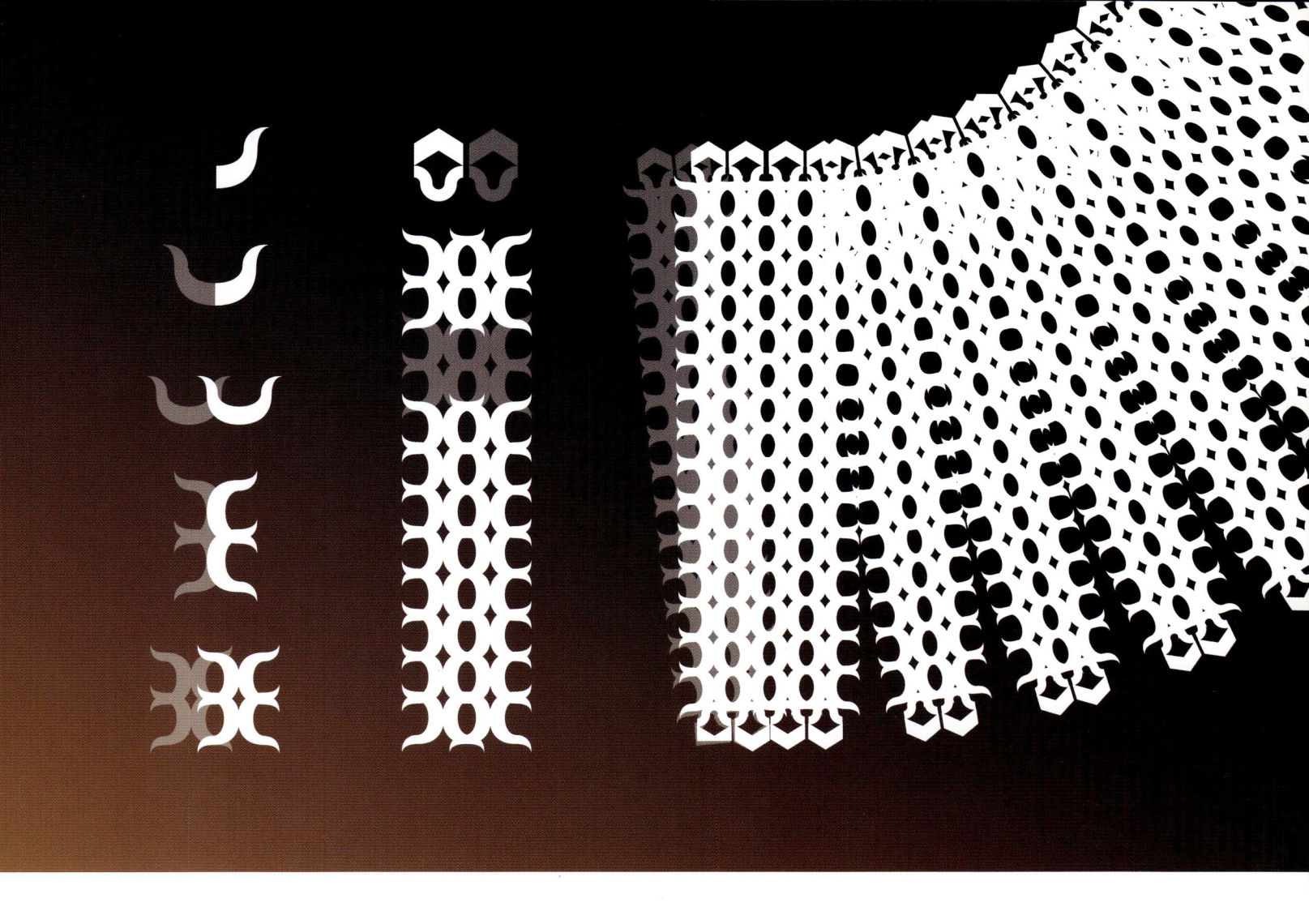

I DID NOT want to limit this illustration to a theme or even a precise subject matter. Before I began working, I decided that I would continue in the same artistic direction as my work in the studio. As usual, my priority was the aesthetic effect of the shapes and lines in an original creation.

I decided not to use all of the available Elements. For example, I got rid of the overly round shapes such as the Bar and the Wurst. They just did not fit in with my illustration style. As for the rest of the Elements, I created new shapes by amalgamating them or grouping them together using the tools available in Adobe® Illustrator®. I also wanted to keep some of the Elements intact and position them randomly in the illustration in a more or less obvious way.

The first step consisted of selecting the original Elements which would be used in the final image. Next I transformed some of them to assemble new ones. For me, this is a very important step of the process, because these new shapes make up the main graphic ingredient of the composition. I spent a lot of time combining, grouping, dividing, and connecting the Elements to make up a palette of graphic possibilities with the new shapes. Once that work was done, I assembled the main part of the illustration using a repetition of the new amalgamated shapes, then arranged blocks of colour, trying to find just the right balance between the lighter and darker tones. As a final touch, I added some of the original Elements such as the Badge and the Cobra to give the final image a visual balance.

I tried to use the same approach as I do when I work in the studio, where I spend the most time and effort finding the right shapes. I did not use my usual method, pixelisation of certain parts and typographic work, because of the limitations given to begin with.

"As a final touch, I added some of the original Elements."

The main challenge for me was to communicate my trademarked graphic style. Secondarily, I was mindful of obtaining new shapes to correspond with my vision because the original Elements did not exactly correspond with my graphic style. However, when I compare this illustration with others I did, I don't feel that the effect is radically different. The number and diversity of the original Elements eventually allowed me to choose the shapes that would be best adapted for use in the final illustration. On the other hand, the creative process that I used for this project was slightly different because of the technical limitations that I was working with.

The Vormator project was very interesting. This challenge was a real playground for me. I got to experiment with my own creative process within fixed limitations.

Spectrum

designer: Muhammad A Novirwan
location: Jakarta, Indonesia
website: www.ayeystudio.com

Muhammad Akbar Novirwan *comes from Jakarta in Indonesia. He was born in 1985 and is currently studying Multimedia Design. He has worked as a motion and graphic designer in a small but creative production house called Intimasi Production. There, he was involved in their first feature length movie called Abu / Abu as an art director and title designer. He believes that his way of producing ideas and problem solving is the answer to your needs.*

After reading "A Designer's Art" by Paul Rand, I found that repetition often plays an important role in building remembrance and memory in one specific design piece. This piece is my attempt to demonstrate the technique. The colours that I used were meant to create variations and to avoid the boredom of repeating geometric forms. The outcome of this piece made me think that colours and forms are important in design. And in my personal opinion a form doesn't always have to follow its function.

I used transparencies to blend all the colours that I have used to create rhythms and also repeated shapes to create patterns and unify the piece. But to avoid the boredom of repeating forms, I did rotation and scaled some of the forms to enhance the variety of my piece. I only used two Elements and from the experimentation of scaling and rotating these Elements, I created new forms. The colour palette was influenced by the spectrum of light. The different colours were intended to create a fun looking design and interest the eye.

"The colour palette was influenced by the spectrum of light."

The piece was developed by taking photographs and doing some sketches. I tried to combine the colours from the photographs and drawings from sketches, and develop them further until I came up with three optimal ideas. And from these three optimal ideas I chose one final idea that was later developed in a digital environment.

Normally when I create a design, I carry out research about the project itself. But in this case I skipped the research process and just did more sketches and scribbles on the idea. I experimented more with combining forms and colours.

I think that the first challenge was to find the right combination between colour and form. Basically, to combine the two used Elements into one fine composition. The second challenge was the amount of limitations in the brief. These pushed me to engage in a more creative process.

I think that the Vormator project has indeed influenced me. Although research is an important thing in a design process, I think that doing more sketches could help a lot in developing an idea too. I believe that a good concept can come from the unconscious mind.

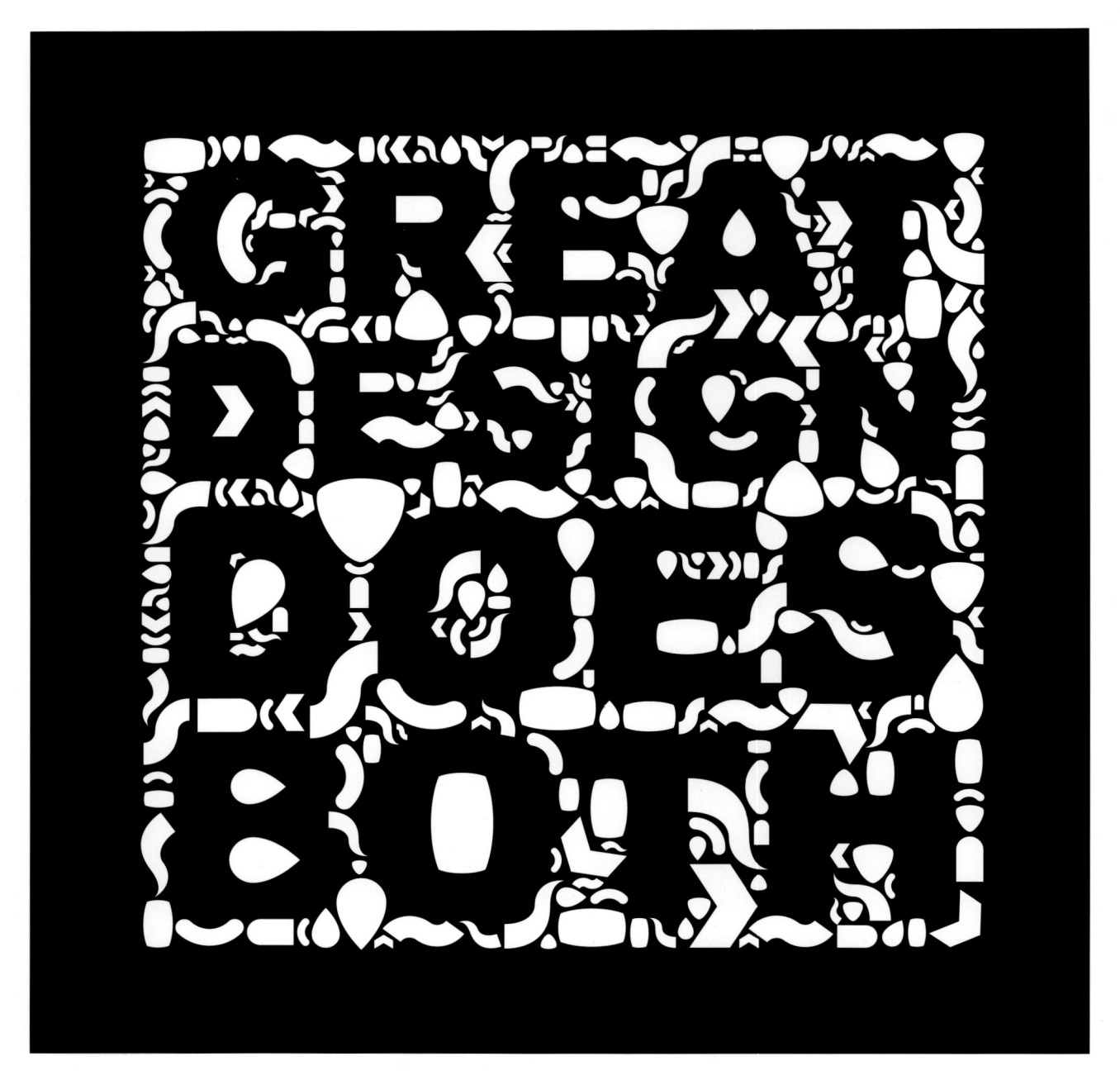

Great Design Does Both

designer: MWM Graphics
location: Portland, Maine, USA
website: www.mwmgraphics.com

MWM Graphics is the art and design studio of Matt W. Moore. Living by the motto "Range is conducive to growth", Matt has worked hard to constantly evolve his craft in the various disciplines of design and art. He received a BFA in Design and New-Media from MECA. He also attended design and illustration classes at SCAD and RISD, and marketing and copy-writing classes at Boston University.

Matt's career path has led him through various creative roles including: gallery artist, clothing designer, screen printer, pre-press designer, editorial illustrator, identity and logo designer, print and interactive designer, art director, web designer, curator, producer and publisher. Each of these experiences has helped to mold Matt into a versatile and prolific creative. Matt publishes a book of personal illustration work each winter called Black and White Bangers, and he also founded and curates the popular website and sticker swap, Wallspankers Magazine. Matt, his wife Laura and their son Malachi live in the mountains of Vermont.

For me, a great graphic must be functional and aesthetically pleasing. This witty statement is my attempt to express the need for both form and function in visual communication.

"I started big and worked my way down to the smallest crumbs."

Some of my favourite works are the perfect combination of information delivery and aesthetic flair. It can be a fine line to walk, but when achieved, attractive and engaging information delivery is unstoppable.

This piece was brutally simple to create. Through the use of scale and rotations I attempted to create a cobblestone look... with the negative space revealing the statement "Great Design Does Both". Most of my design work deals with many layers of shapes and colours. It was an interesting challenge to work in this two dimensional, monochromatic fashion.

It felt like I was building a big vector mosaic, constantly shuffling through my pile of bits in search of the perfect shape to wedge in each little gap. Much like the process of a stone mason, I started big and worked my way down to the smallest crumbs, all the while attempting to achieve a well balanced overall spread. I think it turned out pretty good. It would be great to see it come to life as a stone walkway or stained glass window.

The biggest challenge for me with this project was to find the balance between legibility and the scrambled aesthetic. After all, the message is directly calling attention to the need for both aspects to be considered and executed appropriately. I had a blast trying to figure out how I could make the design pop with so few elements and a limited palette.

Funky Flow

designer: Mykola Dosenko
location: Kiev, Ukraine
website: www.myk31.com

Mykola Dosenko is *a young graphic designer, pixel artist, illustrator, animator and an all-around creative person from the Ukraine. He believes that diversity in what you do is a good thing, as long as you can do several things at a high level. His influences range from basketball and videogames (both old and new school) to a whole variety of music genres, especially hip-hop and its four elements. While his work is diverse in styles and technique, there are always certain basic things he tries to convey in each piece. He tries to make each piece colourful, fun, and makes sure that it contains a witty message. Mykola is also the animator behind the music video for DJ Shadow's single 'This Time'.*

> *"I spent two weeks working on another concept that involved a red giant monster with four tentacles."*

THE PIECE I created here is basically a boom box that is floating in the sky, playing some funk and spreading the good vibes. Funk music, together with jazz, soul and hip-hop, influences me a lot. It is therefore no wonder this piece came to my mind. This specific piece was created while listening to bands like Cameo, Kool & The Gang, and Parliament/Funkadelic. The picture is supposed to be fun, simple, and colourful. I think I pretty much achieved that.

The perfect way to explain my process of creation is comparable with constructing something from LEGO® blocks. There are just eight Elements, but there are absolutely no other limitations, so in the end it is actually quite easy. In fact I found it simpler than just drawing something from scratch, because I was able to concentrate on what I wanted to express and not having to worry about how clean or correct the lines will be.

To create the colour stripes I used some simple colour blending modes just to give it some extra pizzazz. The standard align and distribute tools in Adobe® Illustrator® came in handy to organize the equalizer and especially the speaker grid. The only new shapes I created are the circles (made of four Wurst Elements), and the 'bar' (made of two Zerks) that I used to make the equalizer. And the clouds of course were created from randomly scattered Drop Elements. I probably did not use all the Elements, although I am not sure. I did not intend to use them anyway, I just used whatever I needed. Why use each and every one just for the sake of it?

The funny thing is: I spent two weeks working on another concept that involved a red giant monster with four tentacles bringing chaos and destruction to a big city. That idea sure sounded great, but for some reason I didn't like what the picture was developing into. Then one morning I just woke up with the idea of making a boom box with colourful waves coming out of the speakers. The final piece was done in a couple of hours. I find that pretty amusing!

I personally think it's important not to be afraid to scrap two weeks' worth of work, if you know that you can do better with a different idea. Sometimes an idea just doesn't work, and it's better to switch to something else.

My main challenge was to come up with a really cool idea. I always have lots of crazy, interesting ideas in my head. But when it comes down to picking just one, that's where it gets hard. Especially in this project you only get one shot. Therefore the idea can't be just good, it has to be awesome in all respects. That is mainly why I made the switch from a good idea to a great idea during the process.

I would say that it has indeed fortified my belief that design is first and foremost a creative process and one can never underestimate the importance of an idea. Too many people I know have a routinely mechanical approach to design and prefer to repeat the same steps again and again. I have deep respect for people who don't take the easy route and try doing something original.

Fish Happens

designer: Nagash
location: São Paulo, Brazil
website: www.nagash.net

PROFESSIONALLY, NAGASH IS like a duck: he kind of flies, kind of swims and kind of sings, but can't really focus on a single thing. He has worked on projects involving game development, web design, photography, illustration, music, sound effects, video editing, desktop publishing, black magic, events coordination... and eventually decided that he wanted to do it all. He now calls himself a multimedia designer. Nagash has been around since 1980 and works as a creative director in an agency called Space, runs an experimental music net-label called Chateau Des Reves, a fetish party called Luxuria (as DJ and promoter), and makes editorial photos for Madame Sher Corsets, his wife's business.

My piece is a vulgar display of power. This big and evil beast of the sea, terror of the mariners, plays with the life and fate of poor and honest pirates. Goldfish, shame on you!

I am a copy and paste freak, so I like to duplicate and rotate shapes to get what I want – even when it is not the best approach. I used all the Elements, and took care not to distort them. I used transparencies only when necessary – for example on the ship flags and the water drops. The fish scales have all the same fill colour, so I applied gradients to make then distinguishable and to give some depth to the fish. I dislike these screaming gradients, but they do the trick for a soft light.

I began playing with the Elements just for fun. I think my original idea was to draw some kind of octopus, but somehow I finished with a pirate ship. Then I started the ocean pattern, which was kind of boring, and like always when I am working on something repetitive, I got random and splashed a lot of designs at the borders of the main picture. That was when the fish emerged, out of nothing! I came out with the scales texture, and then I just had to finish him. Better luck next time, pirates!

I had a lot of fun doing this piece and it was no doubt a good experience, as I started to think more seriously about this matter of creativity versus limitations. I realize that some of my best work was created under very limited circumstances, both technical and conceptual. This can be frustrating, but can always be turned into your favour, sometimes leading to unimaginable results.

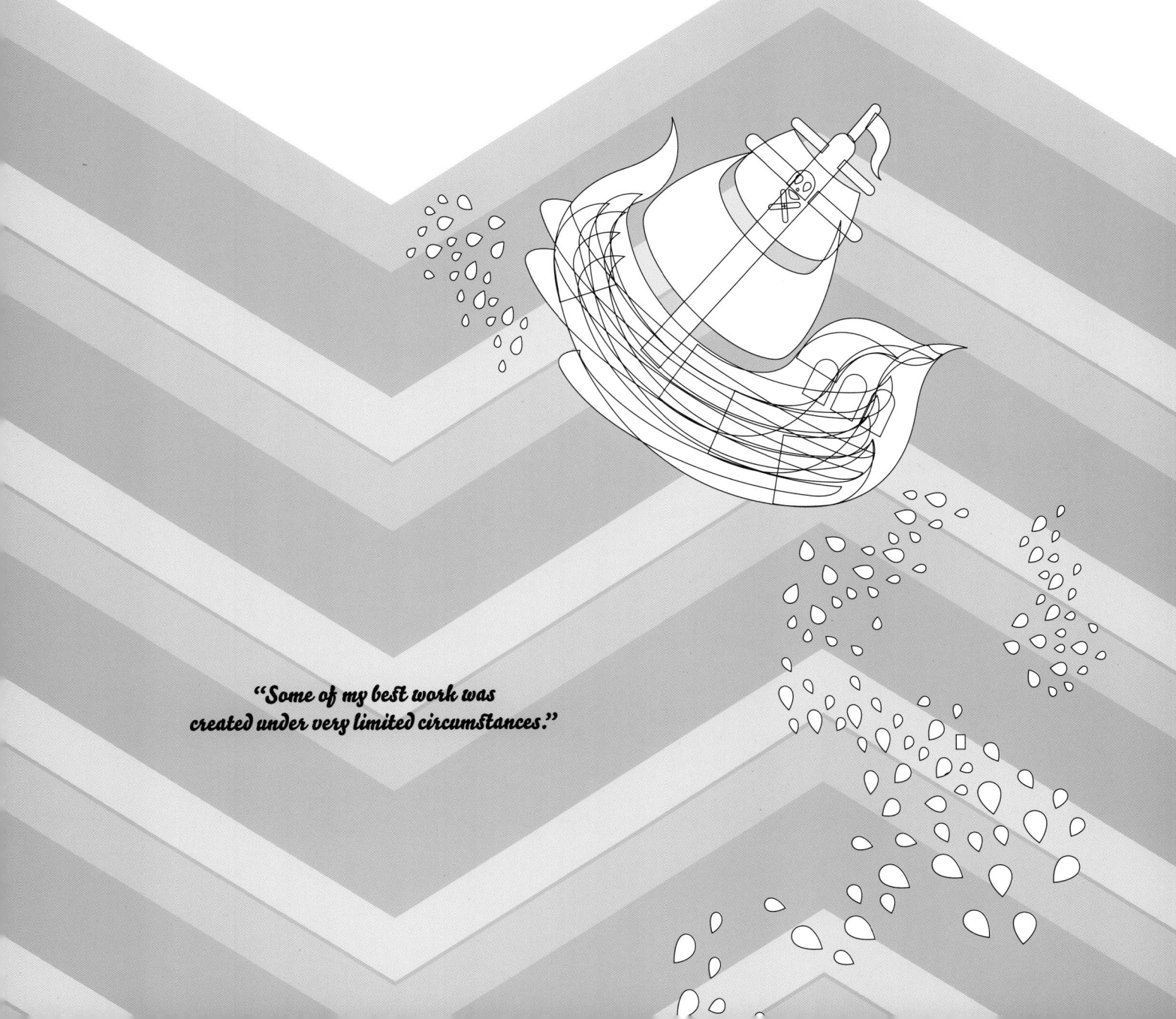

"Some of my best work was created under very limited circumstances."

The Mouse, Mite & Bear

designer: Nathan Cooper
location: Sydney, Australia
website: www.nathancooper.com.au

NATHAN COOPER WAS *born on the 19th of March, 1982. He was brought up on LEGO® and a healthy dose of cartoons. He worked as a web developer, graphic and interactive designer before starting his career as a freelance illustrator and designer in 2005. Drawing is what he loves to do. He likes to draw everything that is around him, as well as creating his own imaginary worlds and creatures. While travelling to and from work, he likes to stare at the sky and watch the clouds drift on by. At heart he is a nerd and he is proud of it.*

> *"Being restricted by the number of Elements that could be used really pushed me to explore many possibilities."*

WHAT IS THIS illustration? That is the exact question I asked myself once I finished the piece. I guess it is a snapshot of the characters that are floating around inside my head on a daily basis.

I simply built up each character design piece by piece by combining the different Elements provided. Firstly by creating the main body shape, then creating either arms or legs or a combination of both. Details were added to give each character unique qualities. I did not use all of the Elements, because each character only required a select few. I did group some of the Elements as this allowed me to create new shapes and forms, which in turn allowed me to develop my characters from such simple basic Elements.

Once I had about 20 different characters I started to layout the simpler ones in order to create a patterned background image. The better character designs were then reworked by combining different forms to create multiple variations of the original characters. I then selected my favourite characters and placed these on top of the background pattern image I had created earlier.

The colour palette for this piece was chosen because of its simplicity and contrast. I also love the combination of blue, black and white as it works very well together. The background was coloured blue, so it didn't overpower the character designs in the bottom right corner, which I wanted to be the focus of the design.

I usually work with pen or pencil and paper before I even start working on the computer. However, for this project I scrapped my normal method and tried something different. I started by working with the vector forms directly on the computer and developing the characters from scratch without prior sketching. I must admit at first I thought it was very hard, however after a day or two I started to realise the potential of this method of character development. Being restricted by the number of Elements that could be used really pushed me to explore many possibilities I normally wouldn't think of.

The development method of starting directly on the computer also formed the main challenge for me. Being restricted to a set number of Elements and having to comply with multiple rules was also part of the challenge for me.

The Vormator project has definitely opened my eyes to the possibilities of restricting oneself when designing, as it pushes the individual to explore different approaches outside ones normal working methods. I will be incorporating what I have learnt in this project in future projects and also develop it further to see what else is possible.

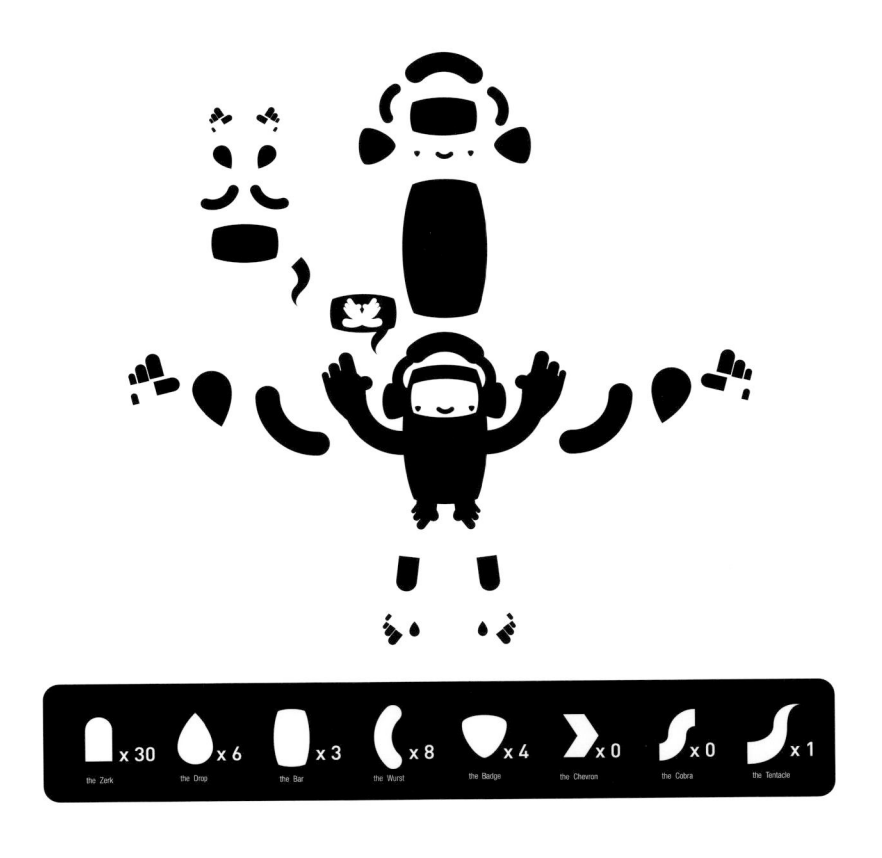

the Zerk	the Drop	the Bar	the Wurst	the Badge	the Chevron	the Cobra	the Tentacle
x 30	x 6	x 3	x 8	x 4	x 0	x 0	x 1

intWo

designer: Orsetta
location: Milan, Italy
website: www.alphameetsomega.com

Orsetta was born on the 20th of April, 1984, in Verona, Italy. She graduated in July 2006 in Communication Design at the Politecnico di Milano, where she continued to study Product Service System Design. She is interested and involved in design, photography and writing. She likes to read, write, listen to music, walk and observe nature (artificial and real) and the silence that there is between all the noises. Orsetta lives and works in Milan.

"My world is communicating with the white space around."

My design shows the world from my point of view. There are gears, the natural elements. It is a private world but there is just one person inside. Maybe there are also some guests. There is a door, and it is locked. It is just an opinion, it is a dream. It is my quiet and dreaming vision of the world. And my world is communicating with the white space around, giving signs.

My first step was to focus on minimalism. I was trying to use as few Elements possible and every Element just once or twice. The second step consisted of thinking about doing something more and to give it a meaning, a concept. Thirdly, I played with the shape created, a circle with many circles inside. This circle was going to be a gear, a part of a bigger process. I then duplicated this shape many times and resized it. At this point I also started playing around with colours. In the fourth step I decided to transform a couple of circles into pieces of the world. I then saw a lawn in these green circles. Finally, in the fifth step I created my vision of the world. I added natural elements such as earth, stones, sky and sun. I also added the door to this world and opened it. The door shows two people inside.

The working process used in this project is different from the one that I normally use. Usually, I think about concept and meaning first, and then I have to find the best shape to express them. In this project the aim is different: to start from many shapes and then find a concept. The main challenge is saying all that by using the same tool. The difference is that it's only a question of a point of view. My aim was to imagine a concept in the union of the Elements.

I found the Vormator challenge interesting and funny. The core of this project, in my opinion, is to give everyone the possibility to say something. I am sure that the possibilities are always infinite, but without tools it is very difficult to express yourself.

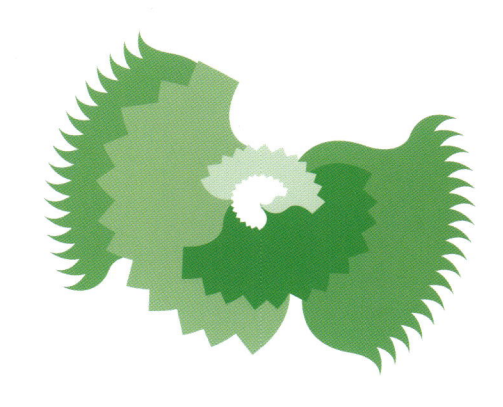

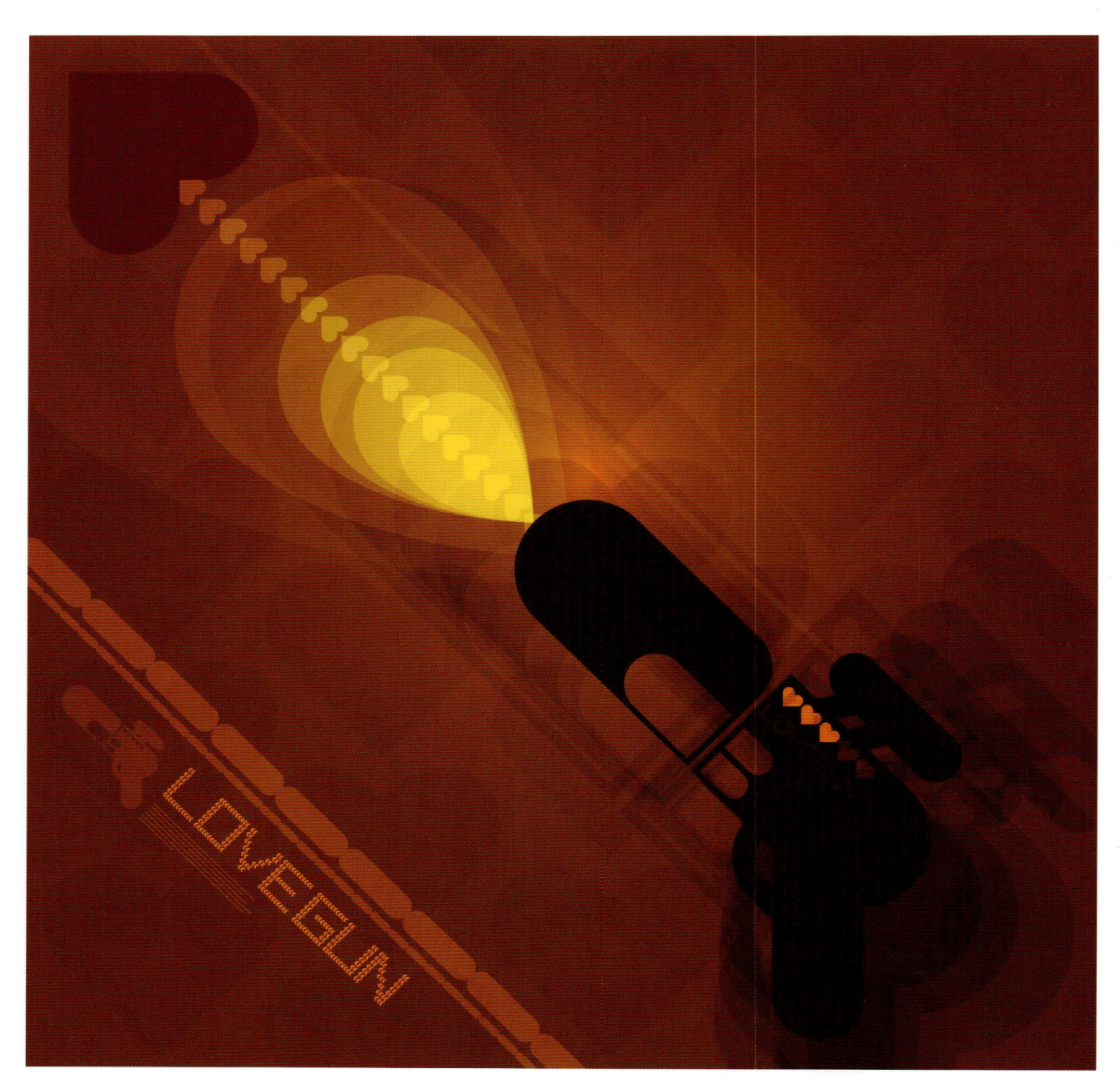

Lovegun

designer: Patrick Kalyanapu
location: New York City, New York, USA
website: www.singlepixel.com

FORMALLY EDUCATED IN *Industrial Engineering at Northwestern University, USA, Patrick Kalyanapu left his knowledge of microeconomics and differential equations behind to pursue a career in graphic design in 1999. He has spent the last five years working at R/GA, doing interactive and motion design for clients such as IBM, Levi's, Subaru, Verizon Wireless, and Nokia. He has also worked on a number of independent projects over the years, most notably for clients including GettyImages, Hard Rock Hotel, Herman Miller, and Travel+Leisure Magazine. In 2005, his directorial debut "Make or Break" finished among the top 15 films in the AAFilmLab 72 Hour Film Shootout and was screened at the Asian American International Film Festival. In 2006, he was a quarter finalist in the NYC Cut and Paste live design competition. In his (limited) spare time, he enjoys living life and documenting it on his rich media blog, introversion.com.*

My piece was a shot at representing the inherent complexities of love and relationships, specifically with regard to the bi-directional nature of giving and receiving, aggression and submission. Does it feel better to give or receive? To enforce your will over another or to submit to the pleasure of your lover? To be selfish or selfless? Are there winners and losers in love? What are we in it for?

I initially approached the project from a micro-level and gradually expanded into a more macroscopic view. By that I mean that I began with combining the Elements to form the basic building blocks that I would use in my design, before actually solidifying my final concept. It quickly occurred to me that I wasn't interested in using all eight Elements, and ultimately I ended up using just three, with one instance of a fourth.

The first and primary basic shape I formed was a heart using the Zerk Element. Shortly thereafter I devised the concept and began creating the Lovegun itself. I wanted it to be highly detailed, yet simplistic at its core. I therefore resorted to primarily using just the Zerk. The only other Elements employed were the Wurst (once) and the Chevron (twice). Given the phallic nature of the gun, the Drop seemed to me to be the obvious choice for the exploding emanation from the Lovegun. I found it interesting that the very same heart shape could be used for soft, juicy lips and sharp, piercing projectiles. Lastly, I felt the title itself should be in the design, as if this were an advertisement for a Lovegun, and the Chevron lent itself well to creating the type.

The use of transparencies was integral to the design. By layering multiple Drops with transparency mode set to overlay, I was able to achieve the effect I wanted for the exploding gunfire – specifically, an integration of both extreme brightness and sense of motion. To further convey the feeling of motion, I created multiple larger-scaled layers of the gun with transparency mode set to soft light. The overall feeling of motion was especially important to me, since I wanted to bring my passion for motion graphics into the equation, adding another layer of distinction to the piece.

My working method in this project, as is usually the case, was determined by the particular assets and constraints that I needed to work within. However, the beauty of this project was that I was able to pursue whichever direction I chose, which is rarely the case with my client work. I find it most enjoyable to create when I have an opportunity to "freestyle" and just let my imagination have free reign.

The greatest challenge for me was in trying to create a unique piece, despite using the exact same Elements that all other designers would be using. So instead of emphasizing the shapes themselves, I wanted to focus on the interplay between the shapes to convey the dynamics in human relationships. I wanted to give the impression that this was one specific moment in an ongoing engagement.

The Vormator project has served as an impetus for personal creative rejuvenation. Having been immersed in a stodgy, corporate world in recent months, it has felt good to get back to my roots and create for art's sake, even when working under various limitations and parameters.

"Given the phallic nature of the gun, the Drop seemed to me to be the obvious choice for the exploding emanation."

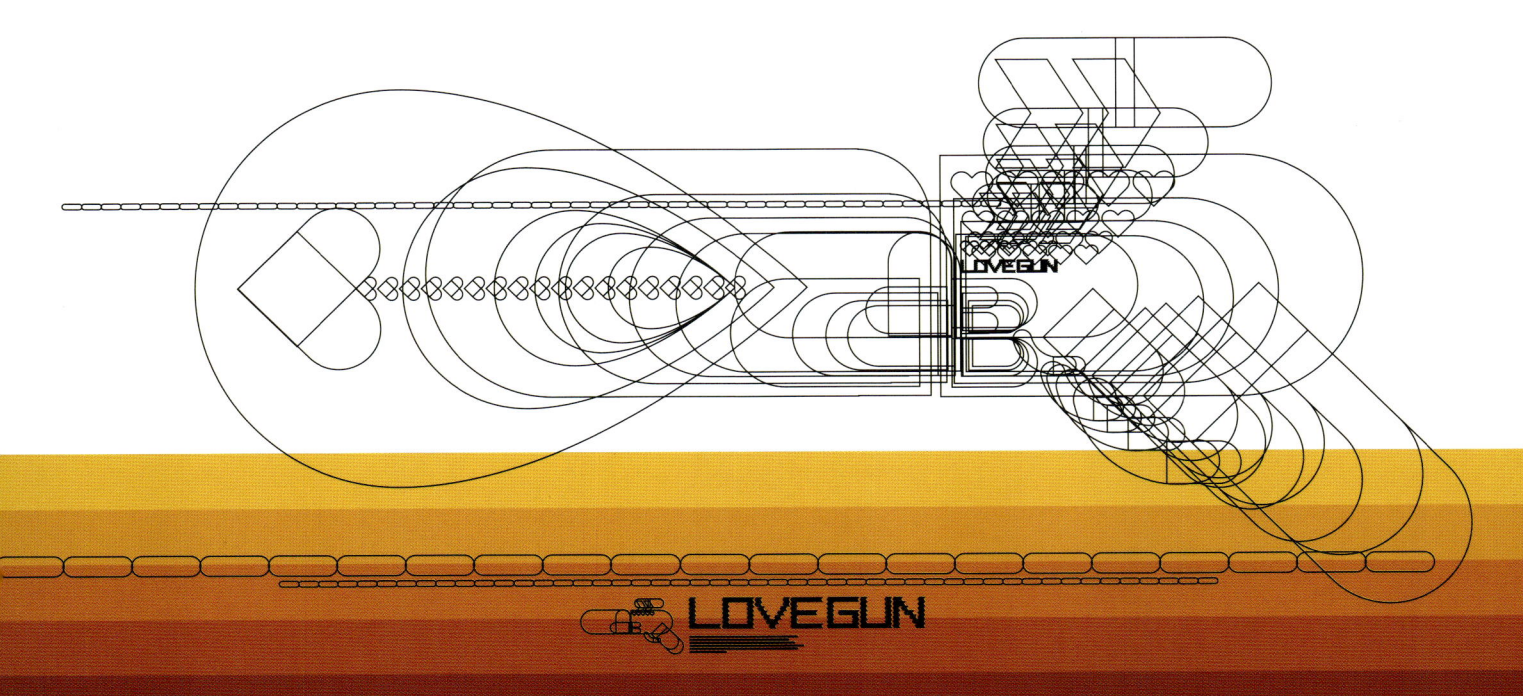

Yarilo

designer: Philippe Sokolov
location: Moscow, Russia
website: www.designsokol.ru

PHILIPPE SOKOLOV WAS born in 1989 in Moscow, Russia. From 1997 through 2006 he studied at the Moscow Art School, Tsarytsyno, where he received basic art education and skills included drawing, painting, composition and art history. In the autumn of 2006 he entered the Moscow State University of Printing Arts, where he is studying at the moment.

SINCE THE AGE of fourteen he remembers being interested in design, in particular graphic, furniture and product design. Young teachers who had just graduated from the leading Moscow universities specializing in graphical and product design taught him the design basics. Besides these subjects, he is also interested in photography and making pictures and is starting to study the subject professionally at University. During his free time he does freelance design work.

THIS IS THE ornamented symbol of the sun. It represents the pagan spirit of old Russia, with its multiple gods and divine beings. One of those divine beings was Yarilo, which is the old-Russian word for the Sun. Every circle of the ornament was made to resemble old-Russian ornaments to the maximum extent possible. However, with use of transparencies and many colours it has a direct connection with modern times. Since it also includes non-Russian features of the Vormator Elements, the symbol can be interpreted as representing the mixture of different cultures and time periods.

First I created circles of different diameter, all aligned by each other's centre and the centre of the artboard just to see how much space each kind of ornament would take. This was important for the overall look and visual clarity. I then filled just one little part of every circle with its specific ornament to see how the finished work would look. I tried many different kinds of ornaments combining Vormator Elements in different ways. When I was satisfied with the result, all I needed to do was to finish each circle of the ornament.

Every object in Adobe® Illustrator® has a centre on which it can be rotated. If you move this centre to a different location, the object will rotate around this new location. I placed the centre of each Element to the centre of the art board and rotated a copy of each many times until all circles were closed. All these steps were done in a black-and-white mode in order to focus more clearly on the form. When the main form with its ornaments was completed, I removed the guide circles created at the beginning and applied the colours.

I used transparencies to make my work more sophisticated. Placing one transparent Element against another gave me the ability to create additional forms. I also created new forms by grouping Elements together. While the main forms were being created, some counter forms also emerged. A counter form is basically a form of a non-occupied background.

In creating this work I was inspired by St. Basil's Cathedral in Moscow's Kremlin, which considerably influenced the overall colour composition. I even took some of the colours directly from the image of the cathedral by using the Eyedropper tool. At the same time I deliberately limited the colour palette in order to preserve the overall clarity. Every ring of the ornament has the similarly coloured "twin-ring" located elsewhere in the layout, which is essential for any good colour composition.

My usual working method is quite different from the method I have used in this project. Usually I create my designs from very different bits and pieces and very rarely use any similar shapes except for typographic ones. In other words, for this particular project I used many more copy-and-paste commands than I usually do. However, the general form of the symbol to be created in this project was round-shape, which is common to many of my works. I use plain vector graphics in almost all my works.

"While the main forms were being created, some counter forms also emerged."

Dragon in Love

designer: **Qian Qian**
location: **Springfield, Missouri, USA**
website: **www.q2design.com**

QIAN QIAN, BORN in 1979, is a multi-faceted designer from China, working in print, web, and motion. One of the "20 under-30 New Visual Artists" of 2006 by Print magazine, he has worked with a wide range of clients, including Nike, Panasonic, Shiseido, and Motorola. His work has been published and exhibited internationally.

"I just played around with the shapes like a child, and along the way my illustration took shape."

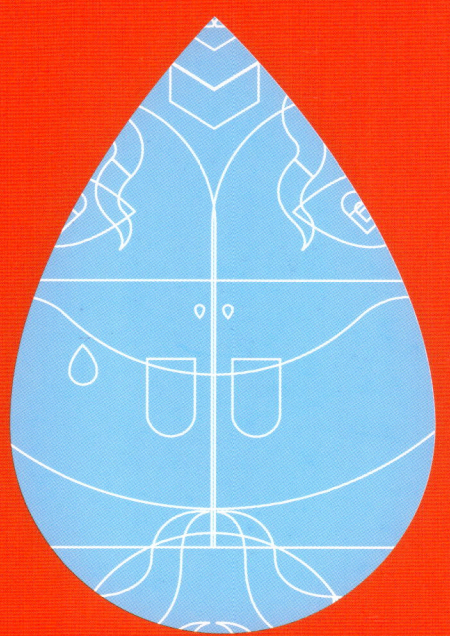

MY ILLUSTRATION DESIGNATES a spring dragon who lives in Springfield, and who starts springing when he feels the coming of Spring.

Basically, the only technique I used to create the shapes seen in my design was to combine the given Elements. In doing that I created new ones in the process. The bright and contrasting colour palette I used was chosen to show that the dragon is excited and in love. I did all the work on this illustration in Adobe® Illustrator®. I just played around with the shapes like a child, and along the way my illustration took shape.

Usually, when I work, I prefer to create forms from scratch. But sometimes I also create new forms out of basic geometric shapes, which is in a way similar to the process for this project.

Working on the Vormator challenge made me believe even more in the aesthetics of geometry in design. I did not feel challenged, but had fun doing this.

10002

designer: Roberto Christen
location: New York City, New York, USA
website: www.mor8.com

ROBERTO CHRISTEN WORKS *as a freelance designer in New York. He makes things for fun and also for money. After he obtained his BS degree in environmental sciences at the Florida Institute of Technology he started to work in the graphics field. He has pursued various projects in screen, print, interface and icon design, as well as interactive and illustration assignments. An Italian-born Peruvian raised in many different places, he likes to travel and prefers simple things over fancy things. Roberto lives in Manhattan with his wife, Charlene.*

"I decided to amplify the project's restrictions by picking a single shape."

MY DESIGN SIGNIFIES a telephone area code superimposed over a rough skyline of the city in which I live. While the city can seem grim and even brutal from afar, the colour and texture found within its streets make this a place of beautiful contrast that pulls you in.

To create the image, I constructed a grid using one of the Elements and started building the same way I did with LEGO® as a child, ANSI/ASCII artwork later, or pixel art even later. I avoided combining shapes or using transparency, but I did use a solid background behind the full composition. Using vibrant colours over duller ones provided the necessary contrast to create depth.

I decided to amplify the project's restrictions by picking a single shape. I used the chosen Element (the Chevron) as the building block to create a mosaic of interlocking Elements of exactly the same size. With all the shapes in place, I began to study themes and colours. Type is an important component in my work, and here it became the centrepiece.

My normal working method often changes and can involve heavy planning... or none, letting the work emerge without a strong focus at the outset, as in this piece.

The biggest challenge in working within a restrictive framework like this is to successfully create something that pulls the focus away from the restrictions or – better yet – something that has merit without evidence of those restrictions.

Great Beards

designer: Sa'd Khorsid
location: Karachi, Pakistan
website: www.flickr.com/photos/100kr

SA'D KHORSID WAS born in 1986 in Karachi, Pakistan. He never really liked going to school, but did show some interest in art. In 2000, at the age of 14, he left school and commenced studying from the safety and privacy of his own home. In the same year, he obtained a computer and witnessed the burgeoning design scene on the internet, which left quite an impression. Working with the speedy enthusiasm of youth, he taught himself to use design software such as Adobe® Photoshop®, Flash® and 3D Studio Max®, amongst others. He began working in earnest whilst studying for dreaded exams. In 2004 he helped setting up a friend's design company. He started to work there, but resigned after just a month, as full-time work clashed with his studies. Taking a practical approach, he took a break from his studies and freelanced for two years before returning to study-mode in 2007.

"The last beardee doesn't like being parted from his tea."

My piece represents five manly men who have great big beards and one great bald head. They seem to be very happy for some mysterious reason. First we have the leprechaun-looking person with an orange beard and a green hat. Then we have the eastern fellow who has read many books and written plenty more. They are followed by the Viking, who likes making two pony-tails from his big yellow beard. Then there is the one with a moustacheless beard. His white cap reflects sunlight, keeping him cool. And finally we have the last beardee, who doesn't like being parted from his tea.

When I started working on this project I tried to use as few shapes as possible, but ended up using all the Elements except the angular Chevron, which I could not really put to any use in this piece of mostly round and curved objects. I just rotated and moved the Elements around, adding and subtracting one from another and creating a couple of new forms with them. I kept on looking for the sides and corners I needed and grouped them together. For example, for the green hat I used the Bar Element and split it in half and attached two Zerks. The teapot is made using three Elements: the Badge for its body, the Cobra for its neck, and the Zerks for its handle.

I started out by making the faces for all the characters (they all share the same head). Then I added a kind of beard. I made several characters at this point and they didn't really fit on my canvas, so I had to pick the most unique ones and got rid of the rest.

My usual working method involves drawing on paper, sketching all the ideas and then moving the whole to ye olde faithful computron. For Vormator I jumped directly on the computer from the beginning, and started playing around with the shapes, searching for ideas (I didn't have a clue at this point about what I was going to make). So maybe after ten minutes of making silly things, I started doing a face, gave it a man-sized beard and tadaa: I got my theme. From then on I searched for great bearded people on the internet and tried to imitate their beards using the Vormator Elements.

The main challenge of Vormator was to make something using only the given Elements and nothing else! What about, say, an ellipse? No. A rectangle? Nope, nothing. We weren't even allowed to use any words! Also the fact that the rules of this project were so simple made it a kind of sub-challenge to not get carried away with the shapes and go crazy.

Working on Vormator reminded me of my nursery days, where we used to make things out of shapes like these. Such as a caterpillar from a bunch of circles or maybe a ship from a couple of triangles, or sometimes even a house from a single square. That made me realize that I can use these old, basic methods in the things I might make. I guess I will try making something entirely of hand paintings in the future.

Sleepwalker

designer: San
location: Hong Kong, China
website: www.wearesmiling.com

SAN, BORN IN 1980, is a game artist and illustrator from Hong Kong, China. Drawing and music are important parts of his life, and he has developed an addiction to character design. Living in a crowded and hustled city, where people live with stress and tiredness, he hopes that people who see his work can experience joy, fun and excitement. He wants to keep smiling, be optimistic and energetic. San is currently enhancing his portfolio and hopes to join projects where he can work together with other artists, designers and illustrator.

At midnight, something huge is coming. It's not Godzilla, it's a sleepwalking monster! The monster walks around and destroys everything around it as if they were toys; it eats everything as food. It is a huge disaster. The city is on fire. Armies ride on fighters to protect their homeland!

There are a number of techniques I used to create this picture. I have combined some of the given Elements with the grouping tool to create a new pattern, such as the body of the monster (combined by the Zerk, Wurst), the monster's map (combined by the Zerk, Chevron and Wurst) and the buildings on fire (combined by the Bar and Zerk and Drop). I have used the intersection of Elements to create things like lightings and shadows, and, for example, the arm of the monster. It is a quick and convenient way to create shadows in vector graphics. Alongside this I have also used transparency to create certain effects, such as the smoke coming from the city and the fire coming from the fighters. Actually, I have used almost all the Elements in the picture (except the Tentacle).

The development of the image can be split into three steps. Step one is the concept draft, this is the first step to create a picture, which is the most important part. Normally, I will make a draft on paper, then scan it and import it to the PC. In step two, the implementation, I used Adobe® Illustrator® to develop the picture. Based on the draft, I outlined the objects and set the colour tone. I used the given Elements, by trimming, intersecting, merging etc., this time to create the picture outline. The final step, optimization, was to add more details in the picture such as shadow, lighting, texture details etc. These features enriched the picture and made it more eye-catching.

In my usual work, I don't set any limitations for myself. I will use my familiar skills to develop a picture, starting from concept draft, then implementation and optimization. But in this project, the major difference is that I had to study the given Elements first and made the draft based on those Elements. It is a new way of working that I haven't used before.

"It was a totally different and new way for me to create a picture."

The main challenge of this project is to create the image using the given Elements appropriately. Since the shapes of the eight Elements are not as common as we are used to (e.g. a circle, a square or a triangle) I had to really think about how to use the Elements, to combine them or to intersect them to create certain shapes, like the pattern on the monster's cap and the smoke effect.

It was a totally different and new way for me to create a picture. It seems that you are unable to make a character (or other shape in a picture) completely freely, but that you can still have a great deal of flexibility. All artists are using the same Elements to create different pictures. In a sense it is just like finishing puzzles, but here every puzzle has its own style and technique.

It was great fun to participate in the Vormator project and it is an interesting way to communicate with other artists.

Las Vormeninas

designer: Sarit Evrani
location: Tel Aviv, Israel
website: sarit.carbonmade.com

Sarit Evrani was born in the beautiful and chaotic Holy City of Jerusalem in 1979. She holds a BA degree in Visual Communications and Illustration from the Bezalel Academy of Art & Design. During the spring of 2005 she studied as an exchange student in the Illustration Department of the Maryland Institute College of Art (MICA), Baltimore. Before, during and sometime after university, she was working both as an interactive designer and a programmer. Her greatest passion in life however is illustration and character design. Nowadays, she focuses her time almost exclusively on doing exactly that.

Sarit works across a wide range of projects, techniques and styles. At the moment she lives in Tel Aviv by the sea. During daytime she works as an illustrator and graphic designer for a leading creative branding agency. In the dark of the night she works on her personal art, listens to music and plays with her real and imaginary friends.

"My main idea was to challenge myself by working as simply as possible."

The piece I created is an homage to Velázquez' brilliant masterpiece Las Meninas. I believe this to be an endless source of inspiration in the history of art.

My main idea was to challenge myself by working as simply as possible, stacking the Elements on top of each other, turning them, duplicating them and playing around with their sizes. I only used low-tech techniques in the process. I have not used any complex manipulations or transparencies due to the same mindset. The colour palette was chosen in order to enhance the bizarre freak show. I aimed for a sickish yet playful ambience in the piece.

Since the composition was fixed and the Elements given, I prepared a palette from the Elements and worked intensively on the design of each character. First, I treated them separately then I placed them together. At this point I went deeper into styling, adding fine details and colours. The process took me one hectic night.

I think that the process and methods I used to create this piece are pretty much the same as the way in which I normally work. I tend to place emphasis on small details and soul. I focus on bringing the character to life, and try to let it stand out of the mass and mess of vectors. Add to this a premium blend of chaos and pure fun, and you are done!

The biggest challenge for me was, as always, the deadline. In the flow of work I found it hard to stop working on this piece. I love experimenting and of course each and every time I do, it has an impact on the way I usually design and draw. The brilliant Vormator experience definitely gave me another lesson on how high one can fly with a set of restrictions and rules.

Vormator Cowboys

designer: Scott Carroll
location: New Orleans, Louisiana, USA
website: www.scillustration.com

SCOTT CARROLL IS *a native of St. Louis, Missouri but has spent his career in the always-inspiring city of New Orleans, Louisiana. In 1995 he decided to leave a small advertising agency to start his own illustration and design studio. This also allowed him the freedom to teach part-time at Loyola University, where he obtained his BA degree in Graphic Arts. Scott enjoys the way in which each day brings something new. Whether it is a spot illustration for the St. Louis Post-Dispatch, a full ad campaign for The National World War II Museum or an exciting new package design for TABASCO® brand Pepper Sauce – his days are always varied. But it has been projects like Vormator that have reinvigorated his passion for illustration and woven new ideas into his client-based work. It is this wide range of fee-based jobs, digital illustration groups and personal fine art projects that keep him happy.*

I view this piece as Clementine Hunter meets Vormator. It is my version of a 1880s Southern Sunday scene.

First and foremost, I decided to use each and every Element for this project. While it was not a rule, I felt it was an important aspect of the project. I grouped but did not blend any Elements. Neither did I use any transparencies because I wanted to maintain a clear, primitive style in the totality of the image. One of the things I wanted to achieve was for all of the Elements to be easily recognizable even when they were combined with others of the same colour. In order to create longer legs I stacked copies of the Zerk. Also, I punched several shapes to create the hat bands, fence, barrel and hay bands, and other forms. I did not use any other manipulations. My decisions for the colour scheme were based on trying to keep the design light and fun in keeping with a primitive folk art style.

Upon downloading the eight Vormator Elements, I printed them out and just sat with them. Pretty quickly, an image of a bull rider popped into my head and I dashed out a quick sketch of half a bull and its rider on the back of some outgoing mail. Step two involved working directly on my computer to create some rough and ready cowboys. I was able to use every Element in my first cowboy. I wanted to have a ton of characters in my final piece, but not wanting them to repeat, I got carried away creating a vast collection of cowboys and their womenfolk. It is like when you use a distressed font on a word like "noodle" and both of the "o"s are distressed in exactly the same way. It rings untrue. In step three, I became obsessed with creating fronts, backs, and different poses for all of my cowboys. I was aiming for a multitude of variations and colours like the 'Guatemalan worry dolls' that were so popular in the late Eighties. The original bull wasn't working for me and somewhere along the way my Vormator Cowboys decided to have a square dance. I slapped the dancers in place and went to bed. The lights had not been off for 15 minutes when the cluttered feel of the final piece was bothering me so badly that I had to get out of bed and create an entirely new piece using the same characters as before. I decided to place my cowboys in a more pleasant environment. I feel that the final piece is much stronger than the original.

There is one main difference between what I did on this project and what I would usually do. Typically, on an illustrative project, I will have a very tight sketch before I start creating the final piece on my computer. In this project, I went from a very loose sketch straight to the computer. I kept the eight original Elements around the art I was creating to help me decide what shape to use next. I also usually try to step away from a project for a while before the final stage of tweaking and improving.

The main challenge for me was to try and create a range of emotions for my characters while keeping the shapes easily recognizable and simple. The Vormator project was a truly fun and inspiring exercise. It has helped me to try and look at upcoming jobs from a new perspective and continually search for a variety of possible solutions.

"I had to get out of bed and create an entirely new piece using the same characters as before."

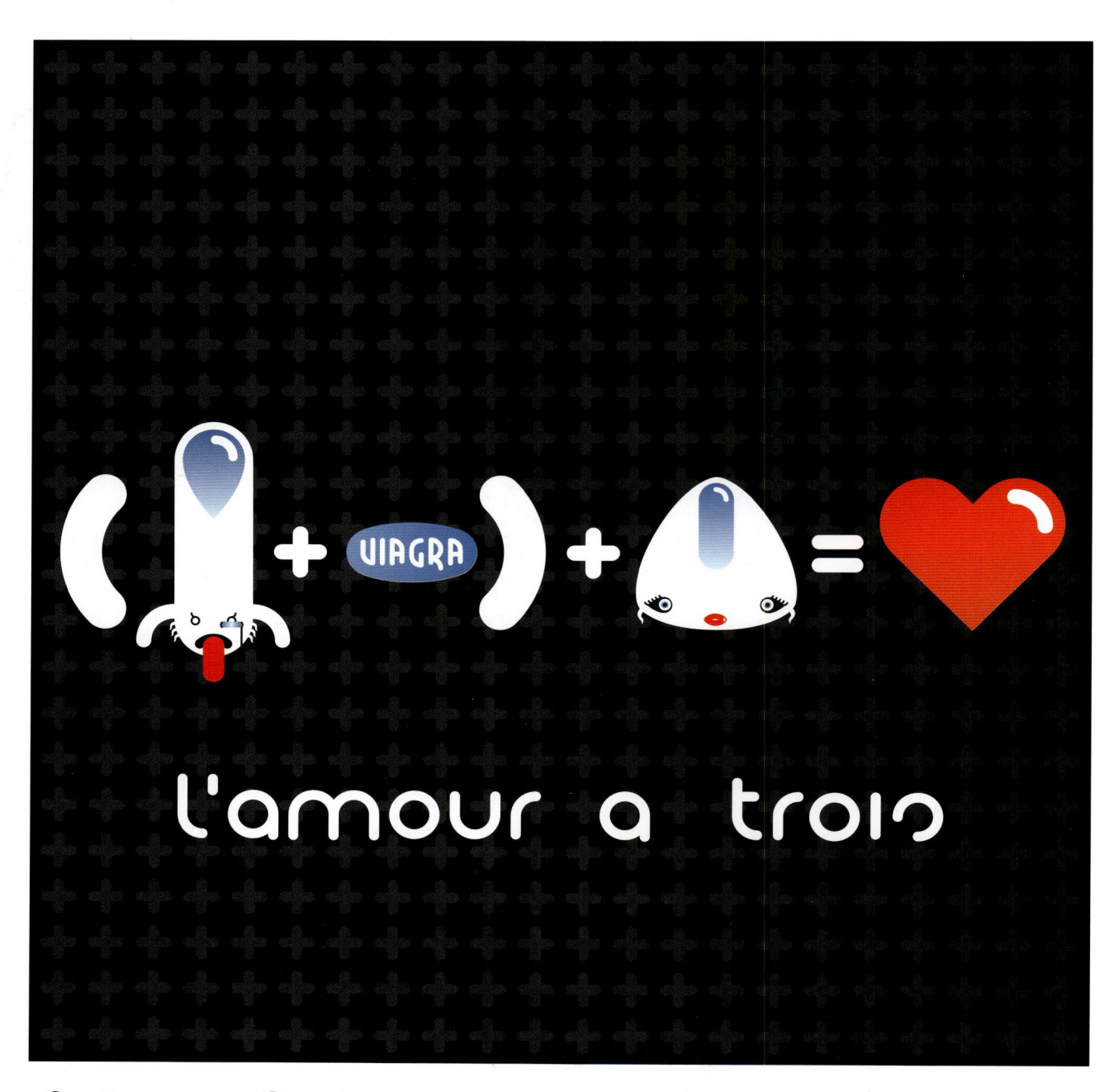

L'Amour a Trois

designer: Stefano Cremisini & Ilaria Conforti
location: Rome/Milan, Italia
website: www.diorg.it

Stefano Cremisini was *born in Rome in 1982. He received his Bachelor degree in Industrial Design at La Sapienza University in Rome. In 2005 he founded Diorg with Ilaria Conforti (designer italiani organizzati) and together they started their freelance careers. Stefano has been involved in a variety of projects ranging from graphic design to interaction and web design. At the moment he is following a Masters course in Communication Design at the Politecnico di Milano University. Stefano now works as graphic and sound designer in Rome, Italy.*

L'amour a trois

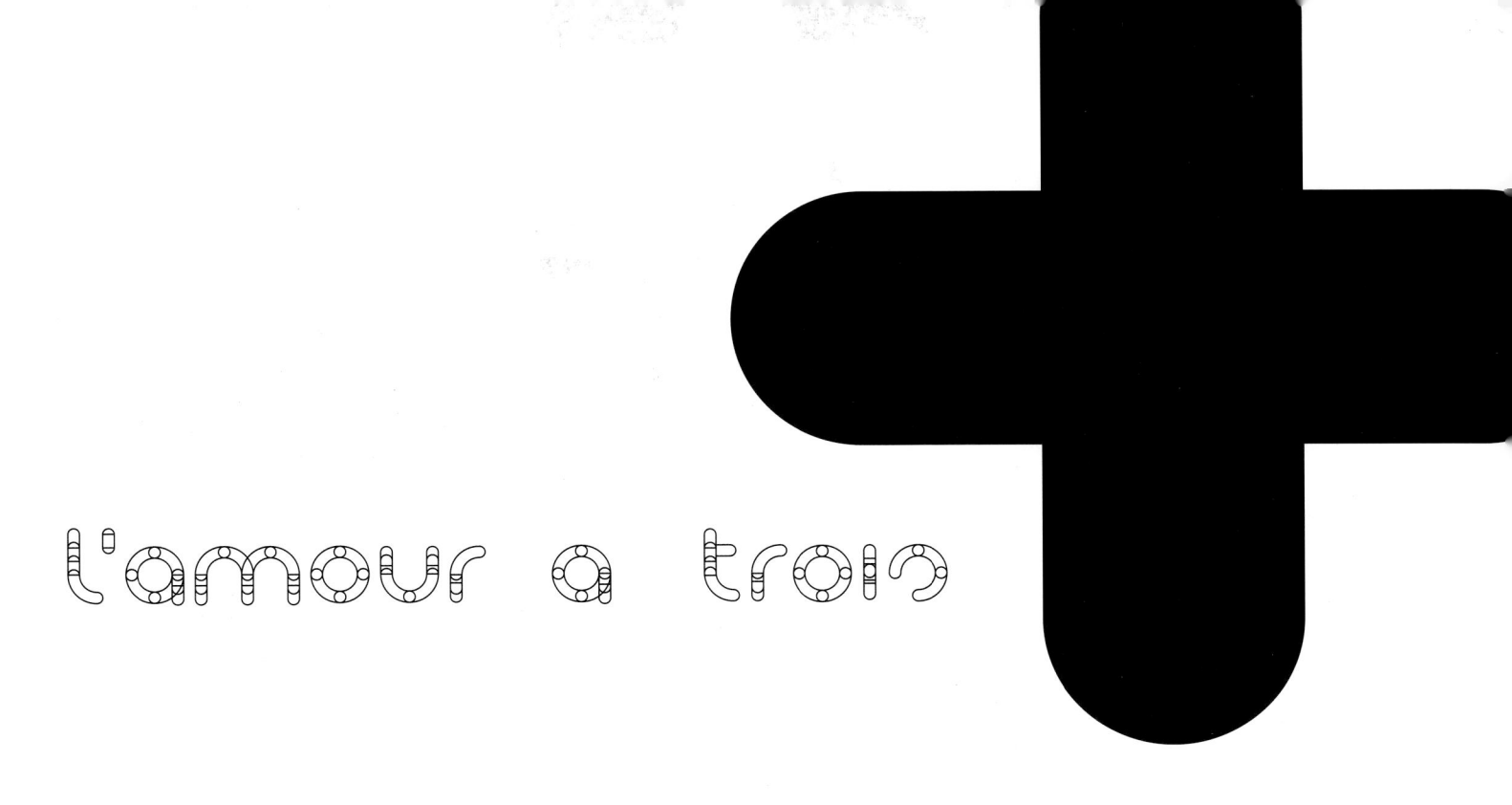

In my design, love is represented through the symbolic images of genitalia, which symbolize both Man and Woman. I wanted to highlight the union of these by the Viagra pill, which in the present day can be helpful to an ageless love.

Through the combination of fixed Elements I started to shape the concept I had thought of. After experimenting with the Elements I got my inspiration for the design I wanted to create. I decided to only use five Elements in total. All these served the purpose of defining a clear image of a mathematical equation: few Elements with different scales, few contrasting colours, and so on.

The progress of my design can be divided into three main steps: Analysis, Combine and Check. I started out by analysing my idea and concept and selecting all the Elements I needed. From these I created the various forms that I wanted to have in my design. I then started to combine these forms into one unique image. In the final stage, check, I verified the clarity of my message in the finished illustration.

> *"The mathematical symbol 'plus' suggested the whole love scene to me."*

My personal approach is basically a scientific or mathematical one, which in a sense relates to the restrictions of the Vormator challenge. The idea for this illustration started from the mathematical symbol "plus", which suggested the whole love scene to me. This is a feature I wanted to emphasise in this work.

I think that the main challenge in this competition for me has been to create an illustration by using fixed shapes. After an initial practice period where I did not manage to control the result, I finally found the right direction in which to concentrate my efforts. I am very satisfied with the work I did.

Rainbow Poo on Stukaworld

designer: Stuka
location: Braunschweig, Germany
website: www.stukabazooka.com

STUKA IS A *graffiti writer, illustrator and graphic artist. Together with his partner and friend BITER he formed the collective Buero|Buero. With their combined strength they colour in the drab monotony of everyday life. Cooperation and fun are paramount for them, however, the quest for world domination tempts them as well. They do not want to reinvent the wheel, but rather aim to contribute to the marvellous world of characters. Stuka operates from Braunschweig in Germany.*

Here comes the Stukaworld. This place is so wonderful. Here we are eating fruity rainbow poo and chilling with Mr. Street and the friendly C, M, Y, K's. Clouds taste like cotton candy and trees like chocolate. Everyone is friendly with everyone else and enjoys life.

In my illustration the given Elements as well as combinations of the Elements were used. It was important for me to let the viewer recognize which basic Elements were applied and I wanted to make sure that they could comprehend the process an Element went through. While designing, only standard options like "unify" or "divide" were used. Nothing spectacular or exotic. In fact the characters and the world originate in my usual stuff and I chose the Elements that fit best in the context. Rainbow poo on the other hand originated from the Vormator basic Element the Wurst. Thanks for the inspiration!

The first step for me was to get the idea for the design. My second step was to start creating the pattern, forms and figures from the basic Elements. I then started creating a world from the results of the second step. And finally I made a party.

Compared to my normal working method this process was much cleaner. For my other work I work in Adobe® Freehand® at the moment, in a rather messy manner. I usually draw freestyle, leaving the anchor points mostly untouched. Afterwards the vector files are pimped in Adobe® Photoshop®. A similarity between my normal working method and the one I used for the Vormator challenge is operating with an archive. In this case we have eight basic Elements and in my archive there are textures, characters, forms and more that I use from time to time to compose my work.

I find it hard to say whether or not the Vormator challenge influenced my way of designing. It is not that important to me. It was a pleasure to create a new tiny world and being a part of the Vormator project. That is it.

Tell your mom you love her smile. Thank you.

"...and finally I made a party!"

Spreading the Vorms

designer: Sven Hendrickx
location: Aalst, Belgium
website: www.sykologic.be

Sven Hendricx was born in Aalst, Belgium, in 1984. He is a young graphic design student at the College of Science and Art, department Sint-Lucas in Gent. Sven has previously studied Multimedia and likes skateboarding, art and playing the drums. As big influences in his life, he believes that these subjects reflect in his work. He remembers loving to draw since he was a small child which, through the years, really hasn't changed a lot, as he likes to create visual eye candy. He really enjoys doing this kind of work and hopes to start working in the graphic design business.

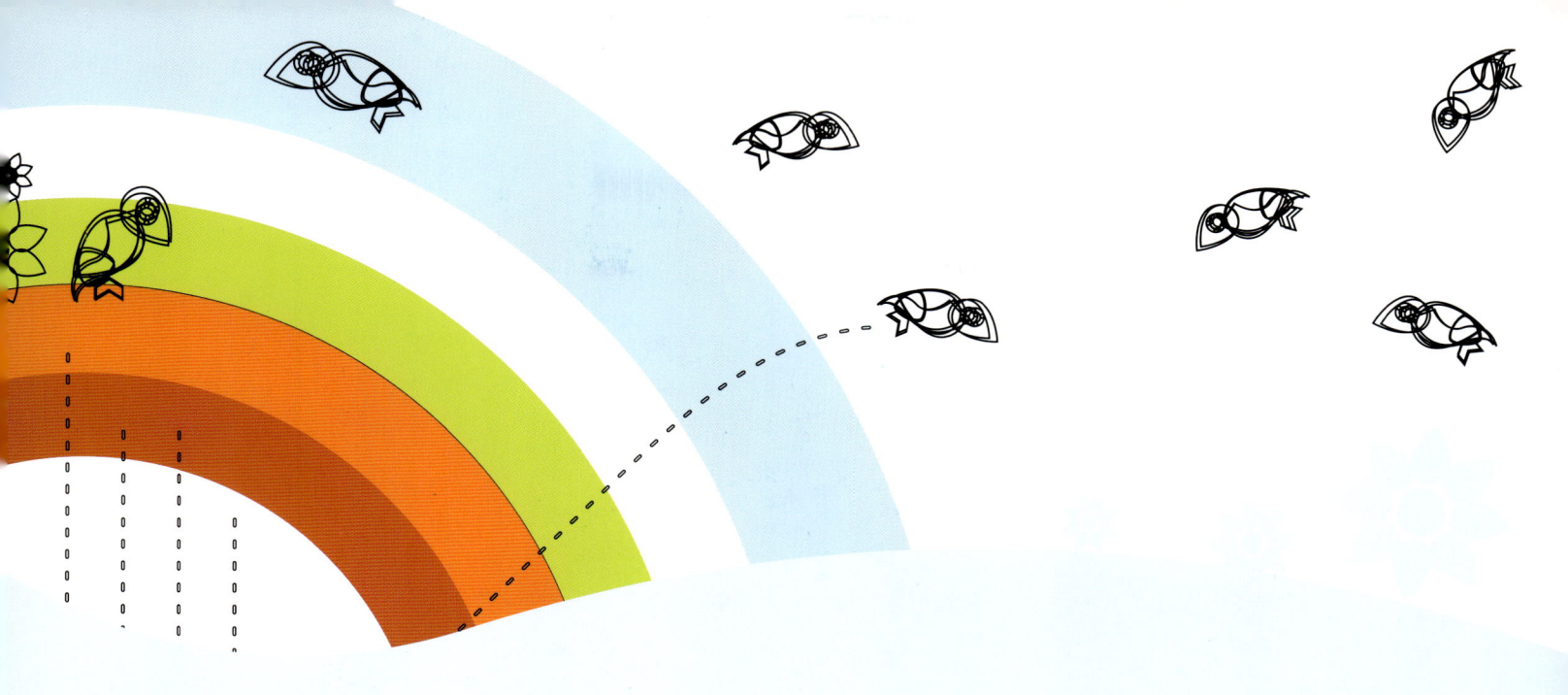

My piece is entitled *Spreading the Vorms*. You can see a Vormator-creature spreading his colourful forms and creativity from the clouds in the sky. I got my idea by asking myself what the influence of this Vormator project would be towards the graphic design community.

I didn't use any complicated gradients or transparencies. I just created some new Elements out of the Vormator forms and grouped them. Then I duplicated them, scaled them, and tried to create a good composition. I probably used every Element, but some attracted me more than others. My favourites were the Tentacle, the Wurst and the Badge.

To create some depth in my work I created strokes behind the more important Elements by duplicating and enlarging the Elements, and then putting them behind the original Element in one different colour. I chose complementary colours in addition to the hard black and white. This resulted in a colour palette that works well together.

After I thought about the subject of my piece I drew the eight Elements on a piece of paper and began to play with them. First of all I wanted to create a character with an unseen 'not-from-this-earth' kind of look. I began messing with the Tentacle because it had the most of these characteristics. Soon I had a complete drawing of what I wanted to create. It was only when I started to create the artwork on the computer that I began to realize that almost anything was possible by using the Elements creatively. But by the time I came to work on the pieces I wanted, some of my earlier decisions on composition and form had changed. So the Vormator Elements did have an influence on that.

The main challenge for me was to create something with simple but predefined forms that still looked like a personal piece. It was absolutely incredible to see the possibilities you have in creating new elements with only the eight Vormator Elements. At the end I'm very pleased how my piece turned out. The most important lesson is that there are more possibilities with any given form than you might first think. This project will definitely help me to be more creative in the future with simple forms.

"There are more possibilities with any given form than you might first think."

Scipione Syndrome

designer: Thomas Moon
location: New York City, New York, USA
website: www.tomodesigns.com

"An artist is what I am, design is what I do." Over the past two years this is the philosophy Thomas Moon has adopted and maintained in his professional and personal work. In other words, there is an environment that guides learning interaction and is a manifestation of pushing the ideals and notions of design. That is what he is searching for. In 2003, after earning a degree in Studio and Digital Arts at the University of California, Irvine, Thomas moved to New York to work as a freelance graphic artist and web designer. Since then he has worked on multiple design projects in a wide range of fields. Staying true to his mantra, Thomas has also continued to explore the realm between his career in professional design and his life as an artist. Since settling in New York, he has dedicated himself to creating original works of art that bridge the gap between graphic design and popular art.

Scipione Syndrome is a reactionary piece on the world of design and its expedient nature of replication. As seen in the image there are multitudes of coloured fish swimming within the endless pathways of black tendrils and tiny penguin like creatures being born from them. The focus was to imply an environment that translates to the new strains of design, always changing and never stopping its continuous evolution into something that becomes inherently necessary with belittled importance.

I began this particular piece by overlapping Elements (in this case a circle) and grouping them together in order to create new forms that were easier for me to identify as a larger mass. Concentric circles became the form that I was most attracted to and seemed to offer infinite possibilities.

I primarily used transparencies, blending techniques and form manipulation to create this piece. Despite the differences between transparency and blending techniques, both were used to create a sense of space. Utilizing the aforementioned techniques, I began to graphically sculpt an environment for the focal point of the piece to inhabit. If a certain technique didn't work, I would move on to the next one, until I reached one that yielded a satisfying result.

Usually when I design, I tend to use shapes that I create from scratch, which are more organic and complex in nature. However, considering the requisite of this piece I tried to explore the potential each Element could offer and somehow blend them into structures that I was more familiar working with. From there I started to remix each of the shapes until I began to compose a structure that closely resembled the blob in my mind. Eventually, as the main creature started to form, the environment simply fell into place in terms of creating an environment in which the form would reside.

Nowadays it is too easy to make a pretty design that is all style no substance, which is why I like building my designs around a strong concept. Once I have my concept down, I begin to loosely sketch a composition in my head. I always keep an open mind while working because more often than not, things change, and sometimes things work better in my head than in reality. This thought process easily relates to the Vormator project as well in terms of thinking of an initial concept even prior to manipulating the shapes provided.

The main challenge, as with my other pieces, is knowing when to stop. The advantage and disadvantage of working digitally is that it is easy to change the composition of your design. By doing so, you're not only opening up new avenues of creation, but also creating new visual problems, which is why competitions such as Vormator allow designers like myself a timeframe to create a finished design: this a challenge in itself.

I wouldn't say that the Vormator competition has changed the way I normally approach a project. However, considering the unique nature of how this piece was developed it has provided a different perspective in terms of how a single shape can have limitless potential in form and function.

"It is too easy to make a pretty design that is all style no substance."

Cheer Up or Die!

designer: Tim Meijer
location: Warrnambool, Australia
website: www.meyerdesigner.id.au

Tim is a young Australian graphic designer with a passion for good design, illustration, photography and typography. A graduate and Honours Student of the University of Ballarat, Tim moved to The Netherlands in 2006 finding work and further education in Rotterdam's design industry. Now living back in Warrnambool, Australia, Tim works predominantly in advertising. His target is motion graphics as well as researching and writing about design.

Cheer up... or die! My piece is about how unhappy people looked sitting on the metro train in Rotterdam, the Netherlands. It's snowing outside and it's gloomy... OK, but it's also beautiful - so cheer up or die Rotterdam!

The scale and layering of the Chevron to get a background was needed as a base. This stack of coloured layers gave the scene a cross section view and everything else worked in line with that. All the Elements were used, nothing was cut or manipulated. Transparent shapes were not needed, although most of these elements do have gradients.

At first I was trying to simply deal with the limitations of the brief, in other words: "what can I do with them then?" Without initial intentions it was a matter of playing around with the Elements to see what could be done with them. From these roughs, little human figures were developed and the metro tunnel idea became clear. The Drop and Tentacle combination for the windmills or flowers were added much later and most of the design was slowly worked on over a few lunch breaks. At first this was all done with a dark and doomy colour palette, just like the weather outside, but eventually I snapped and did the opposite at the last minute. So now maybe it can cheer people up...

Usually I certainly would not put such tight rules on limiting my own artwork, but that is exactly what made the challenge worthwhile. Normally I would be thinking about type and photography or illustration before I start playing around with some random shapes.

I think the main challenge was simply to get the concept I had to work with the shapes and convey the idea within the limitations. A great challenge! I don't believe so much that Vormator has changed the way I design for clients, but it has certainly challenged my process of illustration. Perhaps in time it will be noticeable if it has affected anything.

"Unhappy people sitting on the metro train in Rotterdam, Cheer up or die!"

For Freedom and Devastation

designer: Timo Böse
location: Hamburg, Germany
website: www.lowerground.com

Timo Böse is a 28 year old German designer focusing on motion graphics and illustration. From a background in traditional drawing, painting and street art he started studying Graphic Design in Germany, where he got into computers and digital techniques. He began working as a motion designer and animator while he was still at the university, where he graduated in 2005. Since that time he has worked for numerous clients including Bacardi, BenQ, Daimler Crysler Jeep, Dolce & Gabbana, Funkstoerung, Lexus, Loreal, Nivea and Twentieth Century Fox. He has worked for Agencies in Europa and the United States in the fields of art direction, graphic design and motion graphics. His works have been shown at festivals and exhibitions around the world. Right now he is working in Hamburg, Germany as a motion director. Böse's aim is to keep things fresh by creating his works in many different graphic styles, mixing traditional hand drawn illustration with vector based artworks, photography and complex 3D generated pieces. The inspiration for his works he obtains from frequent travels and music.

My composition of the Vormator Elements is a mandala like symmetric arrangement. My intention was to compose the Elements in a way that will make them look like some complex and organic form. The Elements are part of the whole arrangement without being obviously noticeable. So, the subject was to create a unique, modern mandala from the Elements.

I began by looking at the Elements for some time, moving them around and thinking about what could be done with these fragments. Next I sorted them out and decided not to use all of the Elements, but just the few which looked best to me. Some of the objects seemed to work quite well with each other. I then grouped some of them, reflected and rotated these groups and tried to build basic symmetric groups of the objects. I then arranged these groups to make them look like a single composition and started to colour them in piece by piece. For this I used light and shiny gradients mostly, which I selected visually. When I was satisfied with the result, I started to copy and rotate the newly formed objects to form an overlapping circle. Finally I tried several blending modes to make the single groups fade into another, forming an ornamental circle.

Usually I am not limited to specific shapes when designing something. Of course, there are often guidelines you have to follow, concerning colours, fonts, formats and all that. But working with the Vormator Elements and nothing else was a challenge on its own. So I thought about what to do with the Elements and figured out the possibilities. When I came up with my idea of building this organic form from the Elements I just had to get there. This is a usual process for me: creating a rough visual idea and starting to move things around.

I think that the main challenge was the restriction to use the specified Elements, combined with the fact that all other designers had to do the same. No favourite fonts, no pre-generated graphics, just the few given vector forms. And of course the necessity to do something different with all that.

"It is better to come up with something new instead of using the same footage."

The Vormator project has shown that a lot can be done with just a few simple shapes. It reminded me of the fact that it is better to come up with something new instead of using the same footage over and over. Even when you only have a couple of simple Elements on your canvas, there are still thousands of possibilities to create something unique. That is interesting and should be kept in mind for other designs.

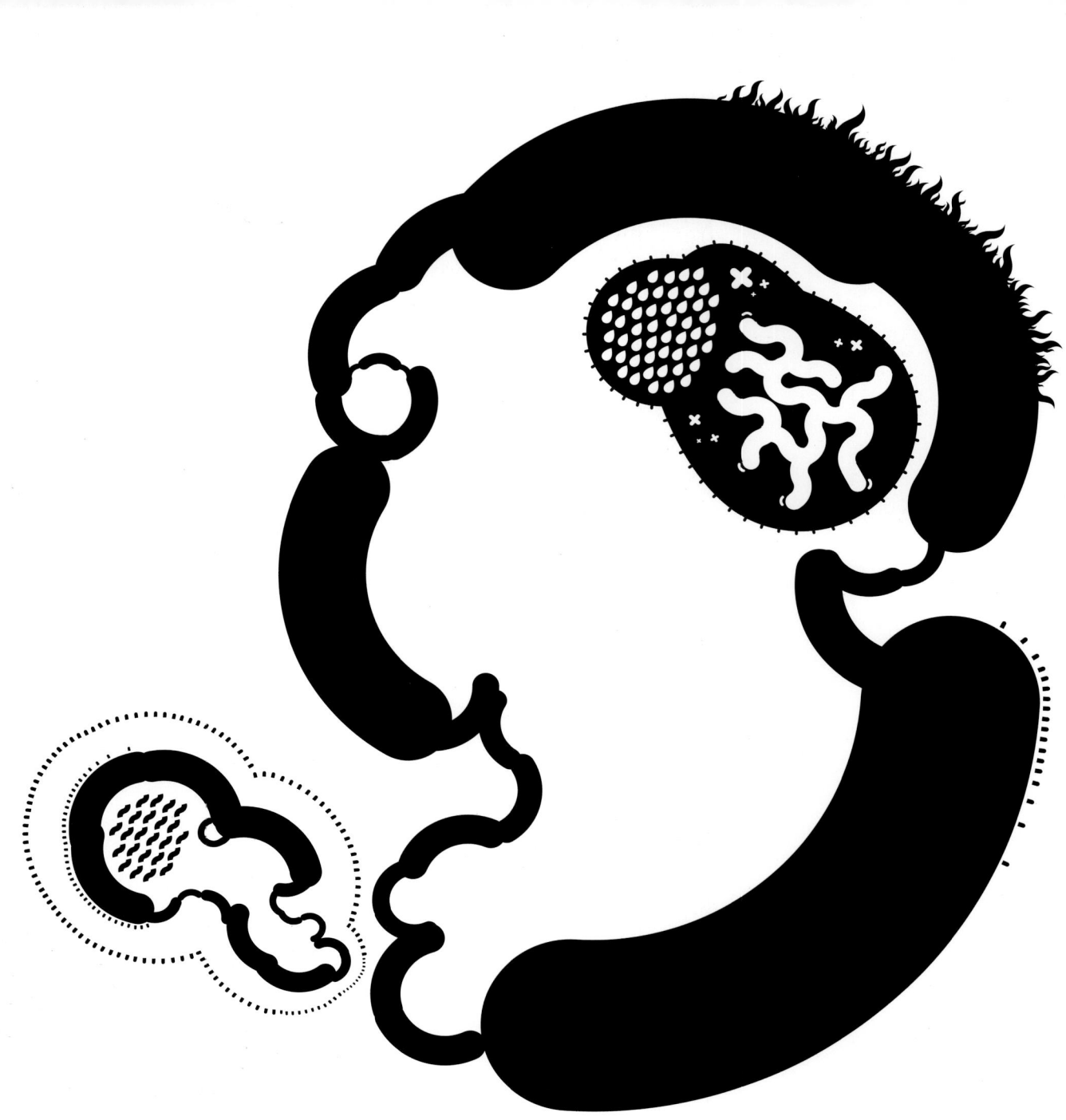

Two Faced

designer: Valero Doval
location: London, United Kingdom
website: www.valerodoval.com

ALWAYS FASCINATED BY *illustration, Valerio obtained a degree in Fine Arts and Design in Valencia, Spain in 2002. He moved from his native country Spain to London in 2004 to study Printing at Morley College. Having received a Creative Futures Awards from Creative Review magazine, he began accepting freelance illustration commissions through YCN and The Creative Corporation. Recent projects include illustrations for Orange UK, Specialten Magazine London, Paul Smith, Volkswagen Spain and some contributions for Pentagram UK, Die Gestalten Verlag and Art Directors Club. Valero Doval currently works as a freelance illustrator and graphic designer based in London, the United Kingdom.*

My design shows two faced faces. One represents us and the other represents our origin, what we were before we had a conscience. Some of the human essence is still inside our mind... one day human beings will be connected with their essence, purifying the negativities of their brains and removing hindrances.

Basically I used just one of the Vormator Elements to develop the main structure of the design. I only changed its size, placing the forms to create the basic shapes and then adding the rest of the Elements to make the drawing more detailed. In the end I only used five of the eight Elements for my design. I did not choose them beforehand, but used them as soon as I considered them necessary. I decided to use only black and white for the colour palette: these are the essential colours in relation to the subject.

Initially, I set out to create a drawing as if it were made by hand. In my usual working method I incorporate handmade drawings, collages and bitmaps and only use vectors for exceptional occasions and this has been one. Within the Vormator challenge I have tried to stick to my personal style while using a different method than usual and the result has been satisfactory. Along the way I chose the Elements that could represent that handmade style. I drew as if I were using a pen, developing the desired shapes then adding small details to create a finished illustration.

The main challenge for me was the contest itself, the concept. It was the capacity to create a piece with my particular style using a limited number of Elements with certain restrictions. This was very attractive to me and I was expecting to do something different.

Working on Vormator has influenced me in terms of process. It is very fascinating to see how different styles and concepts can be developed with the same rules. I think I will use the process I have used here in forthcoming projects.

> *"One day human beings will be connected with their essence."*

FRESH AS FUKK

Fresh as Fukk

designer: Via Grafik
location: Wiesbaden, Germany
website: www.vgrfk.com

"It took a lot of time to arrange all 980 Elements!"

Designer Spotlight

Via Grafik is an art & design studio set up in late 2003. Originally operating as a graffiti crew, they now work as a graphic bureau. At present, Via Grafik consists of the following people: Leo Volland (boe/bstrkt), André Nossek (mnwrks/slave), Robert Schwartz (n6), Tim Bollinger (g13), Till Heim (sign) and Lars Herzig. The Via Grafik design studio is located in Wiesbaden, Germany. Clients they worked for so far are Nintendo, Adidas, Nike, Volkswagen, MTV, Motorola, Opel, Sony, Agfa, to name only the bigger ones!

VIA GRAFIK COMBINES graffiti, graphics and art. On the one hand they specialise in print design, such as logo design, corporate identities, illustration, typefaces, book & catalogue design as well as interior and web design. On the other hand they also work on motion and animation design. On top of these activities Via Grafik operates as an art studio. Every member has a background in graffiti or street art and they are seeking ways to combine their artistic skills with their design skills. In the past Via Grafik has participated in various exhibitions. Even though the members exhibit a great diversity in their artistic visions they continuously manage to combine these in their projects.

By: André Nossek / MNWRKS

I USED A pretty old-school technique to create the graphic, inspired by mosaics. Here one uses a range of elements that only differ in size, and arrange these into the form one wants to achieve. I liked the idea of things being made of smaller things that are also made of smaller things and so on. It is a matter of perception, and you have to look underneath the surface...

I started out with the statement I wanted to use, which is the basis of the graphic. I then got the idea to build it up like a mosaic after which I started to build the design. Since I used the mosaic technique, there was no need to use transparencies and it sufficed to use just one of the given Elements. I wanted to achieve a strong formal aspect in doing so. All I did was resize and rotate the Element: no other manipulations were used. The decision to restrict the colour palette to black and white was inspired by the fact that type is normally also set in black and white.

The method used here doesn't differ that much from how I normally work. Basically I like to analyse a project before I choose the best method to accomplish my idea. The main challenge for me was to keep on working and not lose the enthusiasm and diligence because it took a lot of time to arrange all 980 Elements. This also means that I don't really think this project has influenced the way I normally design. It was a nice project and I liked the initial idea. Fresh as fukk, who doesn't want to be...?

"I often enjoy disturbing the viewer and leaving him with a strange idea in his head."

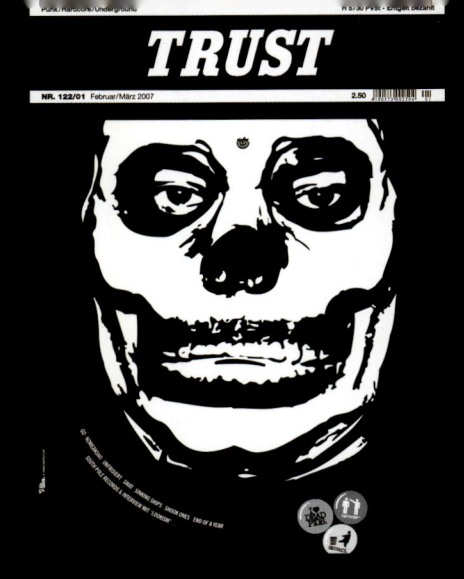

The way I normally work is the following: first of all I develop an idea or a small sketch of the work I am planning to realize. Then I analyse which tool is the best to accomplish the initial idea and start right away. I like the mixture of analogue and digital tools a lot, but the finalization is always done with the computer. I work on a Macintosh computer and mainly use Adobe® FreeHand® and Adobe® Photoshop® for my design work. I often enjoy disturbing the viewer and leaving him with a strange idea in his head.

I am influenced by a lot of things around me, but believe that it can only be seen more subtle in my work since I think copying something is boring. My influences vary from artist like Giant, Wim Crouwel, Dada & Raoul Hausmann, Nietzsche, Sartre, Henry Miller, Refused, Orchid, Delta, Zedz, Coop Himmelblau, Büro Destruct, Luca Ionescu, Monty Python, Herb Lubalin, but also subjects such as sience fiction, chaos and order, love and hate, and so on.

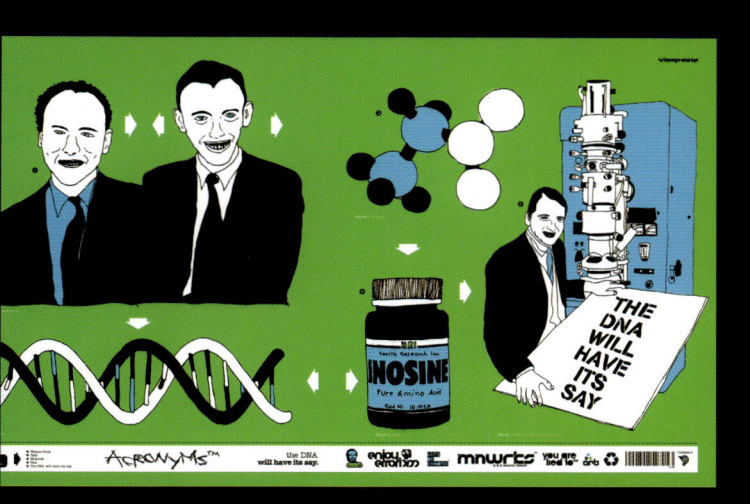

I typically enjoy all varieties of work. I love to design logos, but also planning and executing a mural, setting type for a catalogue or a magazine. Doing an illustration is always nice as well! Clients we worked for so far are Nintendo, Adidas, Nike, Volkswagen, MTV, Motorola, Opel, Sony, Agfa, to name only the bigger ones!

My background in design is that I studied graphic design at the university for applied science in Mainz, Germany. I also did a lot of freelance work in my student time from which I learned a lot. When I finished university, we started the Via Grafik bureau and offered our expertise to the public. I think starting to work for ourselves was an important step in our development as designers because we have more control over the output and also carry more responsibility.

Celebration

designer: Victor Jacobo
location: Compton, California, USA
website: www.vicjacobo.com

Victor was born in Mexico. At the age of 14, he moved to Delano, California, USA, and graduated from high school in 1998. In 2005 he and his family moved down to Los Angeles, CA. where he graduated with a certificate in Visual Communications, at the LA Trade Tech College. He took part in several art competitions when he was in high school. From there he began to realize that he had a talent, which he has been practicing and developing everyday of his life ever since.

This piece is an invitation to celebrate happiness. I decided to represent this composition with children marching and having lots of fun around the beautiful statue of happiness. The children are wearing hats representing a tribute to the statue. They're also holding colourful paper fans in their hands, inviting people to join them and celebrate peace and happiness on earth. I decided to name it *Celebration*, because there are so many horrible things happening in the world right now and our world is forgetting about the things that really matter, like peace, love, happiness, and nature.

As you can see in this piece, I started playing with some Elements by grouping, rotating and overlapping them. Out of these shapes, I started to create the first simple forms such as flowers and butterflies then continued creating more complex forms, like heads and bodies. Finally, I created different layout variations from which I took some of the parts that I've used for the final composition.

> *"Our world is forgetting about the things that really matter…"*

I used a primary colour palette, mixed with dark colours. I've chosen bright colours, which are fun and energetic and a black background that helps the colours to pop up, creating a fresh and unique piece. The shape that I used the most for the project was the Drop and I did not use the Bar at all. I decided to only use a few of the Elements, because I wanted to keep this piece simple and interesting. It took me some time to arrange them all but it was worth it and I really love the final product.

The first step was to choose one or two Elements and start grouping, blending, and rotating them. Next, I chose a blending effect, which blended one shape from small to big, creating a step pattern with different colours. This helped me to set up a style to the piece. After having the style, I began creating the first simple forms. This took me to the next step, which was creating bigger forms by combining and duplicating the first forms that I created. All these steps helped me to develop the composition of this piece.

I used my favourite working method for the piece, starting with simple shapes. This helped me to create new forms and a basic composition in my head. I continued with several compositions by arranging, changing colours, scaling, and rotating all of the different forms that I created. Finally, I combined some of the pieces from the compositions that I liked the most. This approach also guided me to the final layout.

I loved the Vormator challenge because it helped to understand the incredible power of our imagination. Even with just a single shape amazing things can be created that we are not aware of. Vormator helped me to become more aware of the potential that I have. It was a pleasure working in this project.

Kurtz

designer: Visual Data
location: Amsterdam, The Netherlands
website: www.visualdata.org

Ronald Wisse, also known as Visualdata, is a one-man creative studio based in Amsterdam in the Netherlands. His studio focuses both on static and interactive work for print and screen. The work he creates is evenly balanced between commercially orientated client work and experimental personal projects. Ronald has worked on commercial projects for clients such as 20th Century Fox, GettyImages, KPN, Kswiss, Sony and Universal Pictures. His personal work has been on exhibit at the Gogbot festival in Nijmegen, Projector Spectre in Breda and NDSM Kunststad in Amsterdam.

works vice versa: slower mouse movement creates smaller graphics. All in all, this results in a highly detailed graphic representation, further enhanced by utilizing a grid which groups the Elements at set positions on the canvas.

I have been experimenting on and off with the use of Adobe® Flash® actionscript code to reproduce, manipulate and create graphics. The working method here was roughly the same, except for the limitation of only using the eight given Elements which provided an extra challenge. I think that the main challenge here was to ensure the iconic image of Kurtz remained recognisable, while at the same time making it clear that the image is built up out of the specific Vormator Elements.

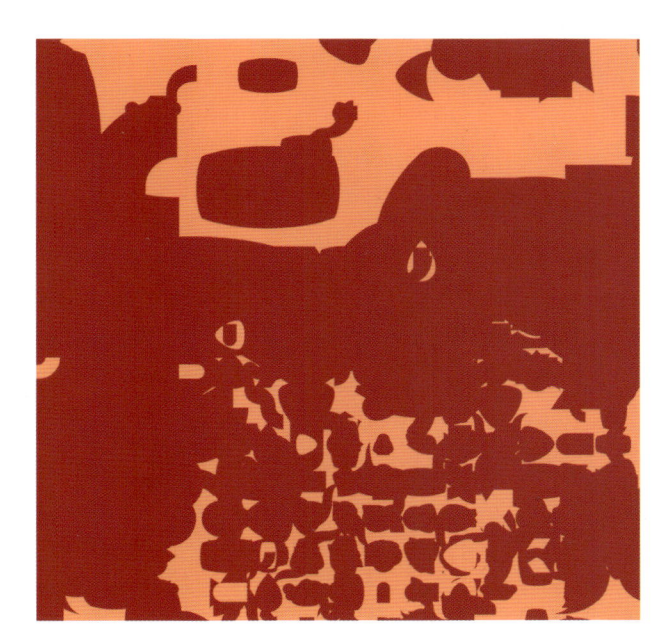

"The main challenge here was to ensure the iconic image of Kurtz remained recognisable."

THE ILLUSTRATION CREATED is a graphic depiction of Colonel Kurtz, one of the characters from the movie Apocalypse Now. The image is built up from of the given Vormator Elements using a record and reproduce process in Adobe® Flash® actionscript code. Using the mouse I hand-traced a picture of the subject twice. The first trace was to be used for the lighter shade and the second trace once for the darker shade. I felt the two colours provided enough contrast in the work, so there was no need to use transparency. Elements were blended or grouped automatically through the technique used, and as a result new forms emerged. I used all of the Vormator Elements in order to get as much variety as possible in the grouped shapes.

The technique I used was the following: while tracing the image with the mouse the actionscript code picks one out of the eight Vormator shapes at random on each frame. By way of storing the mouse positions and tracing speeds inside Adobe® Flash® this allows for the possibility of reproducing the image using the Vormator Elements and manipulating the scale, size and colour of the Elements as a group. The faster the mouse is tracing the image, the larger the graphics produced by the actionscript. This process also

Snap Dragon

designer: Von R. Glitschka
location: Salem, Oregon, USA
website: www.glitschka.com

"He won a contest and was awarded a Speed Racer coloring book!"

Designer Spotlight

Accolades came early for Von. At the age of 5, he won a contest and was awarded a Speed Racer colouring book. That's when he realized a career could be made from drawing. Nothing has really changed...Von still creates award-winning illustration and design, only now for major ad agencies, corporations and national publications, all from his studio in Salem, Oregon. He's given up the footed pyjamas, but in his spare time enjoys driving like Speed Racer in his PT Cruiser. Von Glitschka approaches his projects in the same way using the same methodology, whether it is a professional gig or just a personal one like this.

The actual first step in this process was the determination of a single concept, a main theme. I was inspired by the tribal mask art you see hanging on the walls in museums, particularly that of a Chinese Dragon mask, so I decided to simulate that feel in the art that I created. Knowing I wanted to create a Chinese Dragon mask, I began to arrange my shapes and create a foundation for the artwork. I also balanced my colour palette at this point. The influence of the colour palette in this piece comes from the original image I had of Chinese Dragon art. This art form tends to be very vibrant and colourful so I decided to keep my colours lively.

IN THE SECOND step I started to add detail and created facial patterns by enlarging and cropping new shapes and colourizing them to add more dimension. Having set the right foundation and patterns, I worked in more detail for the teeth and inner eyes. Since this is supposed to be a mask I wanted it to look as if it were hanging on the wall. Therefore I decided to place a background element to act as a plaque. I created the plaque using the 'Bar' shape and then subtracting the 'Cobra' shape from its four corners.

One common attribute in Chinese Dragons are the whiskers. At this point I worked those into the artwork. The other minor detailing work can be found in the gradient radial blends I added in the plaque, inner mouth and center of the face. These additions helped pop out the mask more from the background.

Last but not least, I did all my transparency work: adding subtle shadows throughout the art specifically gives it more dimension and really brings the final piece to life. In my work I tend to use transparency when it makes sense in context of my art.

One of the biggest challenges was that I made a decision up front that I had to use all of the Elements provided. Some are overtly used and one is used very subtly. This was quite a challenge, forcing myself to rely on the raw shapes rather then altering them to the point that it makes using them easier. The only new forms I created were the whisker shapes shown in the art. These were created by simply cloning the 'Tentacle' shape, slightly rotating it from the apex point and then subtracting it from the shape below. What you end up with is a nice sliver of a shape that works as the whiskers for the Dragon.

All in all, I found it a good fit into my existing process and, even more interesting is that I am using this as a class assignment for my illustration students.

"I let each given project I work on dictate the style I feel is appropriate for it."

My design process is pretty methodical. Whether it's purely an illustrative project or a design project I use the same basic methodology. I have documented this process at my illustration website *www.illustrationclass.com*.

My projects are pretty diverse but if I had to pick one favorite it would be illustrative logo design. It's kind of like solving a creative mystery so I enjoy that challenge. A recent project I have had fun working on is developing three brands for a series of TV shows coming out on HGTV. I also created all the illustration work they will be using on the supporting web sites too.

I would say that the biggest influence on my signature style is Jim Flora. He is a 1950's art director for RCA records. You can see his stylistic influence in my work.

Designer Spotlight

In my work, I try to meet the target audiences needs via a clever and fun illustrative design solution. I don't settle for one specific feel or message, but rather I let each given project I work on dictate the style I feel is appropriate for it. That is always the creative challenge.

I've always drawn since I was a little kid. In high school I knew I wanted to pursue art as a career. I attended Seattle Art Institute where I studied Visual Communications and graduated in 1986. Since then I have worked for both large and small creative firms, in house art departments doing both design and illustration. For the last six years I have been operating my own design firm Glitschka Studios and I now refer to myself as an Illustrative Designer.

Repeat After Me

designer: What What
location: London, United Kingdom
website: www.whatwhat.co.uk

TWINS JOHN AND *Edward Harrison work under the name What What. They work together producing weird and wonderful illustrations and designs. Both work in online advertising. What What has been acknowledged by .Net Magazine and The Guardian for its innovativeness. Oh, and they're currently both learning Japanese.*

THE PIECE REFLECTS our interest in repeating patterns. We've created a number of patterns using a similar technique for snowboards and skateboards but wanted to do a pattern with an old feel to it, similar to Victorian tiles and 19th century wallpaper.

The piece was created in Adobe® Flash®. We worked in this way as we've found it easy to create a repeating pattern and to immediately see how it looks as a whole, without copying elements many times. We made an effort not to use any manipulations such as blends or transparencies as we wanted to keep the pattern bold and simple.

We approached the project separately and in different ways. We both played with the Elements, joining them to make new ones, making many more shapes which could be played with. After some time we realized that some of the shapes had become quite intricate and attractive in their own right. We swapped files and began combining shapes and patterns, until, after some final tweaks, we chose a design.

"What What are currently both learning Japanese."

The way we worked on the piece is very similar to how we work on most projects. There's always lots of playing about with ideas until we're both happy, then one of us will usually make a start and whenever that person gets bored or is not happy, the work is swapped over. We find we get the best result this way and the work doesn't become stale.

We've always liked the way certain restrictions help us to be more creative. We often set projects like this for ourselves to see what we come up with.

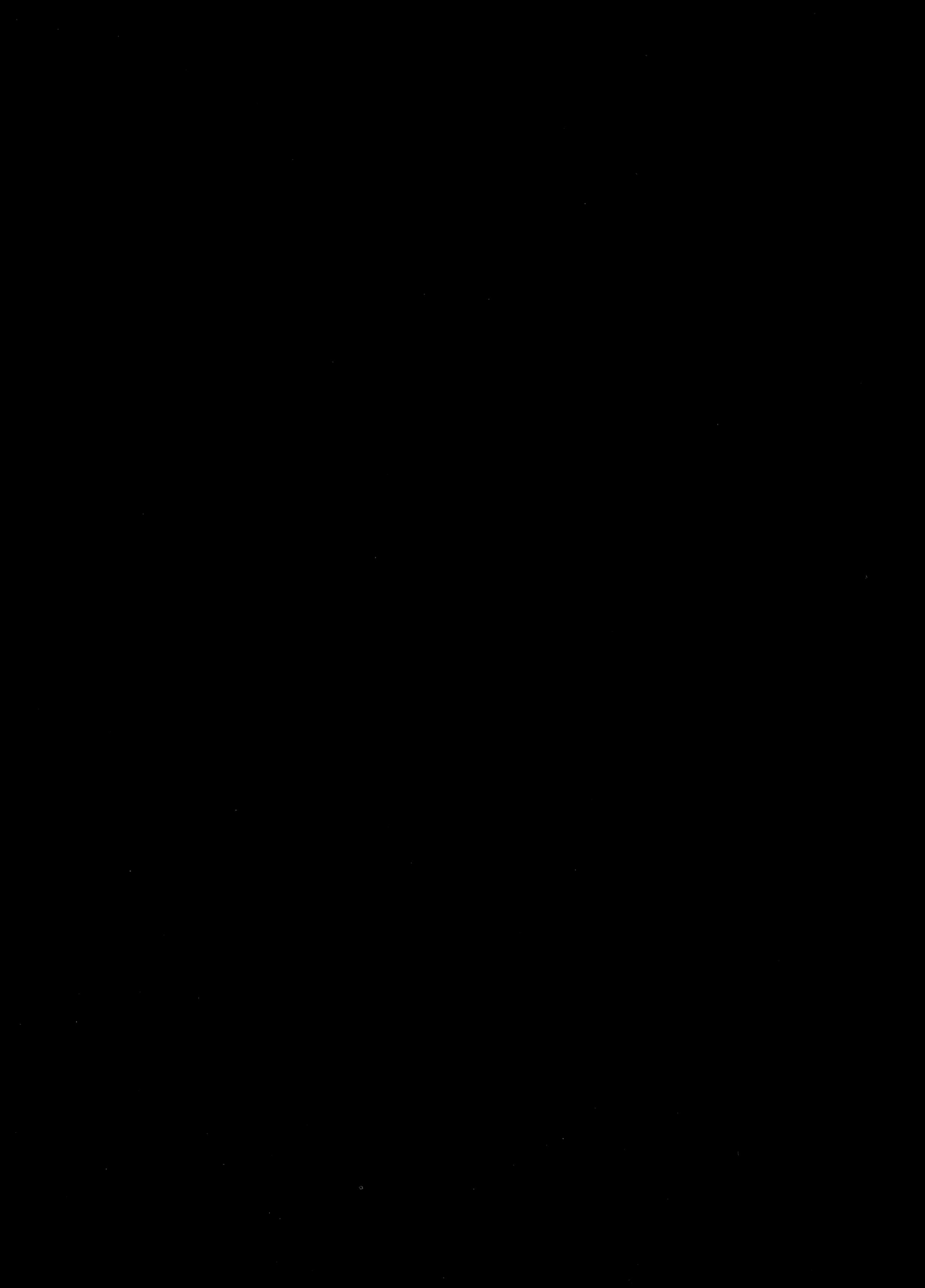

Index

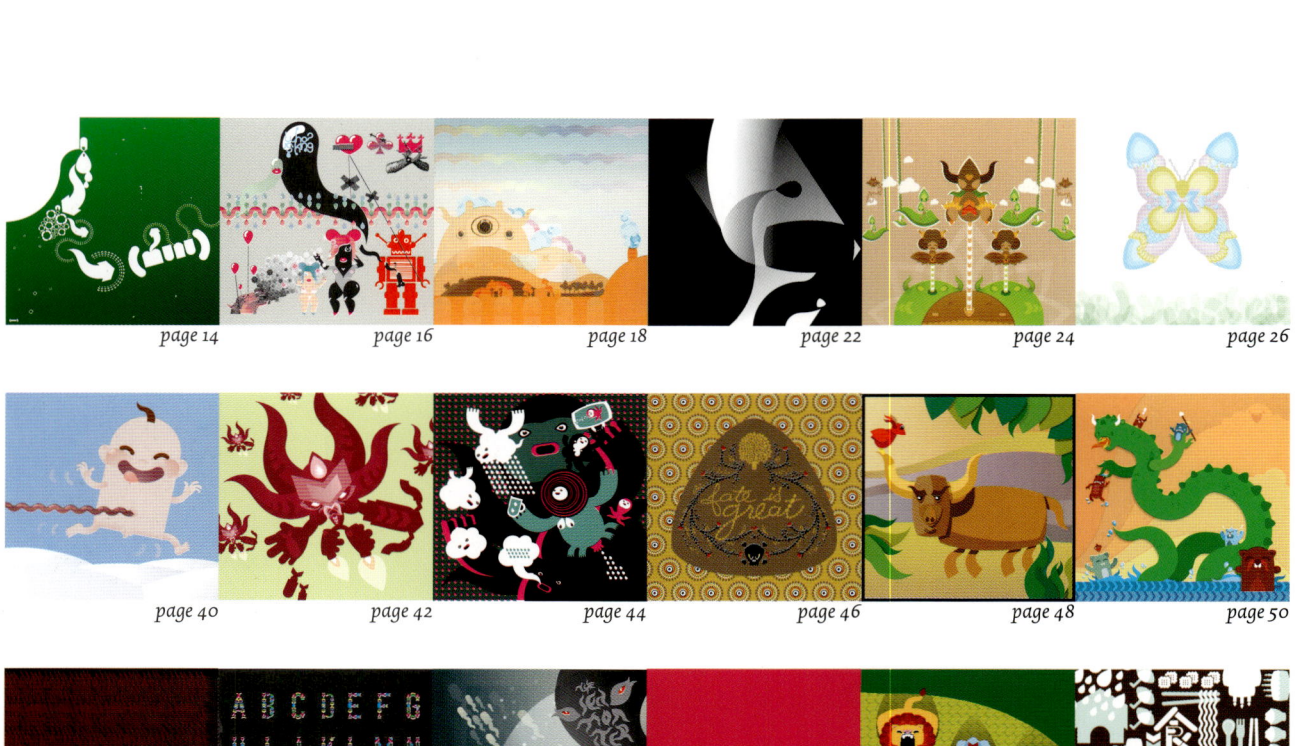

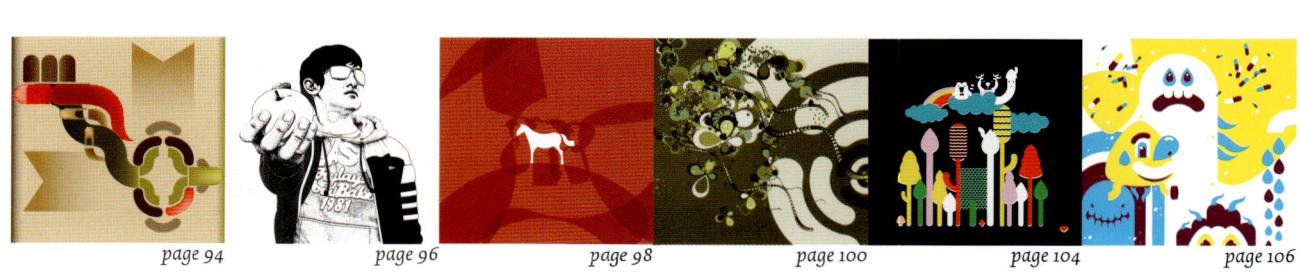

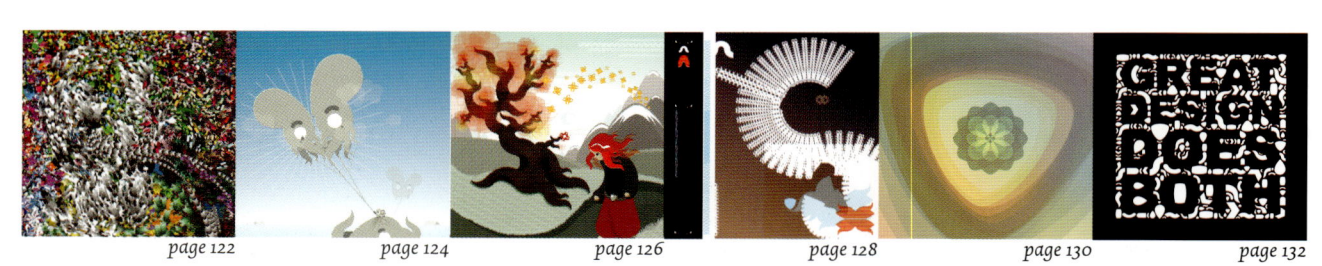

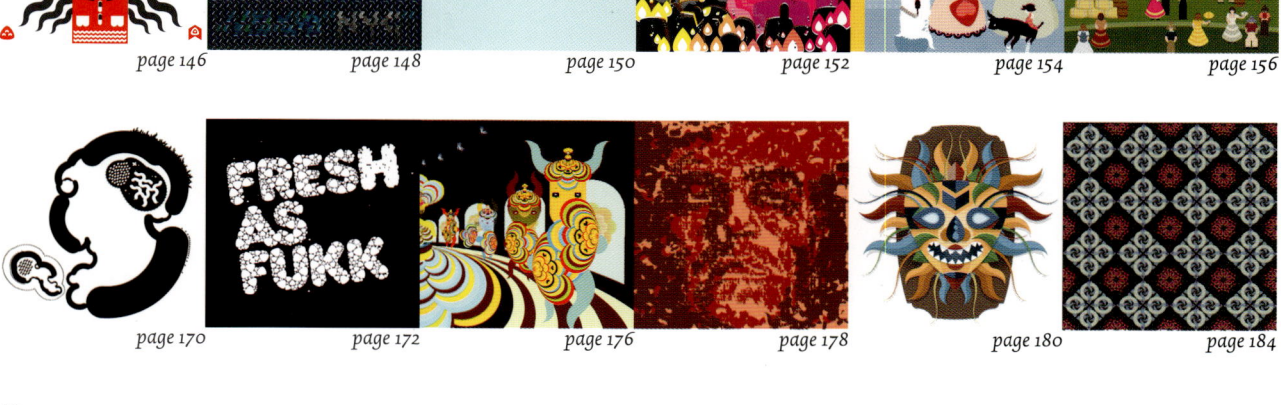

page 14	page 16	page 18	page 22	page 24	page 26
page 40	page 42	page 44	page 46	page 48	page 50
page 68	page 70	page 74	page 76	page 78	page 80
page 94	page 96	page 98	page 100	page 104	page 106
page 122	page 124	page 126	page 128	page 130	page 132
page 146	page 148	page 150	page 152	page 154	page 156
page 170	page 172	page 176	page 178	page 180	page 184

188

page 28 page 30 page 32 page 34 page 36 page 38

page 54 page 56 page 58 page 60 page 64 page 66

page 82 page 84 page 86 page 88 page 90 page 92

page 108 page 110 page 112 page 114 page 116 page 118

page 135 page 136 page 138 page 140 page 142 page 144

page 158 page 160 page 162 page 164 page 166 page 168

189

Colophon

VORMATOR
the elements of design

Vormator Concept and Design:	Booreiland & Zeptonn
Layout:	Booreiland, Zeptonn & Eelke Dekker
Text Editing:	Booreiland, Zeptonn, Textcase & Bart Westerveen
Introduction:	Von Glitschka, www.glitschka.com
Published by:	BIS Publishers
	Het Sieraad Building
	Postjesweg 1
	1057 DT Amsterdam
	The Netherlands
	T +31 (0)20 515 02 30
	F +31 (0)20 515 02 39
	bis@bispublishers.nl
	www.bispublishers.nl
Printed by:	Damiprint China
ISBN:	978-90-6369-197-4
Vormator:	www.vormator.com
Booreiland:	www.booreiland.nl
Zeptonn:	www.zeptonn.nl

Copyright © 2008 Booreiland, Zeptonn, the individual artists and BIS Publishers, Amsterdam

All rights reserved. No part of this publication may be reproduced or transmitted in any form or by any means, electronic or mechanical, including photocopy, recording or any information storage and retrieval system, without permission in writing from the copyright owners.

Thanks to all the participating artists for coming up with such a vast range of outstanding artwork and interesting solutions.

All artwork remains the copyright of the artists. Respect copyright, be creative!